AngularJS in Action

AngularJS in Action

LUKAS RUEBBELKE
with BRIAN FORD

MANNING
Shelter Island

For online information and ordering of this and other Manning books, please visit
www.manning.com. The publisher offers discounts on this book when ordered in quantity.
For more information, please contact

    Special Sales Department
    Manning Publications Co.
    20 Baldwin Road
    PO Box 761
    Shelter Island, NY 11964
    Email: orders@manning.com

    Manning Publications Co.   Development editor: Cynthia Kane
    20 Baldwin Road   Technical development editor: Leonardo Cassarani
    PO Box 761   Copyeditor: Benjamin Berg
    Shelter Island, NY 11964   Proofreader: Katie Tennant
                        Technical proofreader: Richard Scott-Robinson
                               Typesetter: Gordan Salinovic
                            Cover designer: Marija Tudor

ISBN 9781617291333
Printed in the United States of America
1 2 3 4 5 6 7 8 9 10 – EBM – 20 19 18 17 16 15

To my father, Daniel Ruebbelke,
who is the foundation of my life

brief contents

contents

foreword

I realized how awesome Lukas was the day we met at ng-europe. After the conference, we started talking more and I participated in a hackathon he organized, and the other way around. The one passion we share, and what has brought us together, is helping people build awesome stuff. I know for a fact that was the reason he decided to write this book. Not for him, but for you!

AngularJS is quickly becoming one of *the* front-end frameworks to use. It's also one of the most rapidly changing frameworks out there. In this book, you'll learn how you can build an exciting application from top to bottom with AngularJS, while learning what controllers, templates, directives, services, factories, and providers are. Instead of an extensive in-depth guide to Angular's features, in this book you'll get a quick glance at what they are and then get your hands dirty so you can learn by using them! You'll learn not only how to code this application, but also how to test it.

Angello is the exciting application—it uses some of the most interesting libraries out there for AngularJS. It's a project management tool very similar to Trello. Throughout the book, you'll learn how to implement the different pieces of this application, and how to use ui-router, Auth0, and Firebase, among others.

I know you'll find this book really useful. Happy hacking!

MARTIN GONTOVNIKAS
DEVELOPER ADVOCATE, AUTH0

preface

Never in my wildest dreams did I think that I would be an author, and yet here I am. I vividly remember the panic that I felt as I clicked "Publish" on my first WordPress post on AngularJS. It felt like I was pressing the launch button for a series of missiles, and I had no idea where they would go! Little did I know that I had in fact released a series of missiles that would change my life in the most profound and unexpected ways.

The moment I decided that I cared more about being helpful than being perfect was one of the most important turning points of my life. Beginning with a series of barely passable blog posts, by accepting every opportunity to implement feedback I gradually grasped what it takes to write a solid blog post. It was also during that time that I had the opportunity to become friends with the AngularJS core team. AngularJS at the time was still relatively unknown, and so it was much easier to get on their radar than it is now. Lucky me!

I'll never forget that afternoon when I got the email asking if I was interested in writing this book. When I was pretty sure that no one was looking, I would break out into this little happy dance for days. If only my high school English teacher could see me now!

From that moment, I have considered it a great privilege to share with you the things I've learned while building some large applications and writing untold lines of AngularJS code. It's been a most excellent journey, and I thank each and every one of you for making this possible!

LUKAS RUEBBELKE

acknowledgments

This book wouldn't have been possible without the input and support from the amazing AngularJS community. I want to thank Brad Green, Igor Minar, Miško Hevery, Brian Ford, and Matias Niemela for their friendship and for setting such a great example of what it looks like to build awesome things. I would also like to thank Jeff Whelpley, Brandon Tilley, Omar Gonzalez, Martin Gontovnikas, Joe Eames, and about a hundred other people for their feedback. They helped me craft Angello and the book that's built around it. I would also like to thank Geoff Goodman for his contributions on the awesome drag-and-drop example. And I owe Jonathan Garvey a huge debt of gratitude for helping me get this book over the finish line. You are holding this book right now because of his help and tough love. Special thanks to Martin for penning the foreword to the book, and to Brian for his contributions at the beginning of the project.

I especially want to thank my saint of an editor, Cynthia Kane, for her infinite patience, for helping me to become a better writer, and for sometimes nudging me to do things I didn't want to do—like write! Thanks also to everyone else on the Manning team who worked with me during the development and production of the book.

Many people read early drafts of the manuscript and sent in corrections and comments as it was being written, including numerous MEAP (Manning Early Access Program) readers, as well as the following reviewers: Ahmed Khattab, Brian Cooksey, Chad Davis, Daniel Bretoi, Fernando Monteiro Kobayashi, Gregor Zurowski, Jeelani Shaik, Jeff Condal, Jeff Cunningham, Richard Scott-Robinson, Robert Casto, Roberto Rojas, and William E. Wheeler. Thanks to all, with a special acknowledgment to technical proofreader Richard Scott-Robinson, who checked the code and read the manuscript one last time, shortly before it went into production.

about this book

The goal of this book is to equip you, the reader, with an arsenal of practical techniques that you can use in the real world—to help you build a non-trivial web application from the ground up, and offer commentary on the most pertinent pieces. The sample application presented in the book, Angello, comes with a fully functional back end in either Firebase or Node.js with a few extra bonuses such as social logins with Auth0.

We had to make some hard decisions about what we were going to cover in the book and, more importantly, what we would not cover. It would have been easy to go down a rabbit trail as we tried to explain AngularJS on a molecular level, but the actual application of this knowledge is relegated to edge cases at best. We'll be the first to admit that we don't cover everything about AngularJS—that would make for a book three times the size of what is currently in your possession.

We make some assumptions about the readers of this book so they'll get the most out of the material. We assume a fundamental knowledge of HTML, CSS, and JavaScript. We don't call out the CSS or HTML in the application unless it pertains specifically to what we're doing in AngularJS.

Roadmap

We've divided the book into two main sections: a gentle introduction to AngularJS and then an in-depth commentary on the pieces of AngularJS, as we start to build out Angello.

Part 1, "Get acquainted with AngularJS," introduces the high-level pieces of AngularJS and talks about what each piece does and how they fit together (chapter 1). To reiterate these concepts, we build out our first AngularJS application, a simplified version of the main sample application, in chapter 2.

Part 2, "Make something with AngularJS," gets into more advanced and specific topics, such as server-side communication, directives, animations, routing, and forms and validations. In each chapter, we look at the underpinnings of the topic and then see how it appears in the context of a real application. We end each chapter with a discussion on testing and best practices. Chapter 3 discusses how views and controllers work together in AngularJS to control what the user sees, as well as capture user interactions and convey those events for processing. Chapter 4 expands on controllers by introducing services and then showing how to communicate with a remote server using the `$http` service. Chapter 5 introduces directives and shows how directives turn layouts into components while providing complex functionality. We'll kick our layouts up a notch in chapter 6 by adding in animations using `ngAnimate`. Chapter 7 digs into using routes in AngularJS to deep-link to specific states in the application, preloading specific data using `resolve`, and passing variables from route to route using `$routeParams`. Chapter 8 finishes off with a discussion on how to use form validation to enhance the user experience while providing safeguards around the data being entered.

There are also four appendixes about setting up Karma, setting up a Node.js server, setting up a Firebase server, and running the sample app.

Source code conventions and downloads

The source code in the book, whether in code listings or snippets, is in a `fixed-width font like this`, which sets it off from the surrounding text. In some listings, the code is annotated to point out key concepts, and numbered bullets are sometimes used in the text to provide additional information about the code. The code is formatted so that it fits within the available page space in the book by adding line breaks and using indentation carefully.

All of the source code for the examples in the book can be found at this Github link: https://github.com/angularjs-in-action. The sample application for the book is at this repository: https://github.com/angularjs-in-action/angello. The simplified version of the application is at this repository: https://github.com/angularjs-in-action/angello-lite.

You can also find detailed instructions on how to get the applications up and running in the readme file. Visit the repo often for updates and bug fixes to the project as well as bonus repositories.

The source code is also available for download from the publisher's website at www.manning.com/AngularJSinAction.

> **NOTE** At the time of this writing, Angular 2 is in an alpha release and not yet ready for writing non-trivial applications. With that said, we'll be publishing an Angular 2 version of Angello as soon as it makes sense.

Software requirements

To run the sample applications, you'll need to have Node.js installed. You can find the installation instructions for Node.js at this link: https://nodejs.org/. To run the tests, it's also necessary to have Karma installed to execute the unit tests. You can find instructions on how to install Karma at their website: http://karma-runner.github.io/0.12/index.html.

We also recommend installing the serve npm module, a lightweight web server to display your web applications in the browser: https://www.npmjs.com/package/serve.

Resources

- The most valuable resources for the book are the repositories you will find at the link https://github.com/angularjs-in-action.
- You can also see a live version of Angello at the companion site for the book at this link: http://www.angelloinaction.com/.
- And you'll find a ton of helpful material at the blog "One Hungry Mind" here: http://onehungrymind.com/. Additional content relating to Angello, based on reader feedback, will be posted.

Author Online

Purchase of *AngularJS in Action* includes free access to a private web forum run by Manning Publications where you can make comments about the book, ask technical questions, and receive help from the authors and other users. To access the forum and subscribe to it, point your web browser to www.manning.com/AngularJSinAction. This Author Online (AO) page provides information on how to get on the forum once you're registered, what kind of help is available, and the rules of conduct on the forum.

Manning's commitment to our readers is to provide a venue where a meaningful dialog among individual readers and between readers and authors can take place. It's not a commitment to any specific amount of participation on the part of the authors, whose contribution to the forum remains voluntary (and unpaid). We suggest you try asking the authors some challenging questions, lest their interest stray!

The AO forum and the archives of previous discussions will be accessible from the publisher's website as long as the book is in print.

about the authors

LUKAS RUEBBELKE started programming in 2001 when he discovered Flash. He learned to program in ActionScript 1.0, which is a prototypical language. Almost fifteen years later, he has come full circle as he spends almost all of his time writing JavaScript.

Lukas lives in Phoenix, Arizona, where he is passionately dedicated to the community and cohosts one of the largest meetups in the valley. He's also an avid blogger at http://onehungrymind.com/ and has spoken at many conferences, including ng-conf, ng-europe, and ng-vegas. He is completely sold on the belief that programming changes lives, and this book is one of the artifacts of his deeply held conviction.

BRIAN FORD is a developer working on the Angular core team at Google. Self-described as often "the most millennial person in the room," Brian started committing to Angular core while studying Computer Science Engineering at the University of Michigan.

about the cover illustration

The figure on the cover of *AngularJS in Action* is captioned "Man from Vukovar, Croatia." The illustration is taken from a reproduction of an album of traditional Croatian costumes from the mid-nineteenth century by Nikola Arsenovic, published by the Ethnographic Museum in Split, Croatia, in 2003. The illustrations were obtained from a helpful librarian at the museum, itself situated in the Roman core of the medieval center of the town: the ruins of Emperor Diocletian's retirement palace from around AD 304. The book includes finely colored illustrations of figures from different regions of Croatia, accompanied by descriptions of the costumes and of everyday life.

Vukovar is a mid-sized town in eastern Croatia. It has the country's largest river port, located at the confluence of the Vuka River with the Danube. Vukovar has always been a thriving community due to its fortunate location, and it has served as a gateway to Austria and the west for centuries. The figure on the cover is dressed in his Sunday finery—blue woolen pants, a black woolen vest over a while linen shirt, topped by a voluminous black cloak—all richly adorned with the intricate and colorful embroidery that is typical for this region of Croatia.

Dress codes and lifestyles have changed over the last 200 years, and the diversity by region, so rich at the time, has faded away. It is now hard to tell apart the inhabitants of different continents, let alone of different hamlets or towns separated by only a few miles. Perhaps we have traded cultural diversity for a more varied personal life—certainly for a more varied and fast-paced technological life.

Manning celebrates the inventiveness and initiative of the computer business with book covers based on the rich diversity of regional life of two centuries ago, brought back to life by illustrations from old books and collections like this one.

Part 1

Get acquainted with AngularJS

Welcome to the world of AngularJS! Part 1 of this book provides a high-level overview of AngularAS, as well as a gentle introduction to AngularJS through building a simple—yet useful—web application.

In chapter 1 we introduce all the major pieces of AngularJS and discuss what they do and how they fit together. We also introduce a simplified version of the book's sample application and build it from the ground up. In chapter 2 we discuss how to assemble your AngularJS applications using best practices to make sure that your applications are maintainable and extensible.

By the end of part 1, you should have a good grasp of the major pieces of AngularJS and be conversational in how they all work together. If you work through how to build the sample application, you'll also have a good foundation for beginning your AngularJS journey.

AngularJS is a very dynamic and quickly evolving framework, so please reference the repository for the latest code samples as well as bonus content: https://github.com/angularjs-in-action. You can also find the code for the first project here: https://github.com/angularjs-in-action/angello-lite.

Hello AngularJS

1

This chapter covers

- Why you need AngularJS
- How AngularJS makes your life easier
- Understanding AngularJS from a high level
- Building your first AngularJS application

There was a time many internet years ago when any kind of logic within a web page had to be sent to the server for processing and then re-rendered as an entirely new web page. This "call and refresh" arrangement made for a disjointed user experience, which was only exacerbated when network latency was especially high.

The entire paradigm was upended with the introduction of `XMLHttpRequest` and the ability to make asynchronous calls to the server without actually having to refresh the page. This made for a much more coherent user experience because the user could perform a task that required a remote call and still interact with the application as the call was being made and processed. This is where the first wave of JavaScript frameworks landed and managed to prove that working with JavaScript could be done in a mostly sane way and no one was going to lose life or limb.

Most people would agree that jQuery won that round, partially because jQuery did such a good job of abstracting away all of the insanity surrounding browser variations, and allowed developers to use a single, simplified API to build websites. The next frontier was to make websites behave and operate as if they were actual applications; this ushered in an entirely new set of challenges. For instance, jQuery has done an exceptional job of providing tools to manipulate the DOM, but it offers no real guidance on how to organize your code into an application structure. We've all heard horror stories of how a jQuery "application" ballooned out into a monstrosity that could barely be maintained, much less extended.

This desperate need to write large, maintainable JavaScript applications has given birth to a JavaScript framework renaissance. In the last couple of years, a slew of frameworks has burst onto the scene, with many of them quietly fading off into oblivion. But a few frameworks have proven themselves to be solid options for writing large-scale web applications that can be maintained, extended, and tested. One of the most popular, if not *the* most popular, frameworks to emerge is AngularJS from Google.

AngularJS is an open-source web application framework that offers quite a bit to a developer through a stable code base, vibrant community, and rich ecosystem. Let's identify some of the high-level advantages of using AngularJS before we get into some of the more technical details of the framework.

1.1 Advantages of using AngularJS

In this section we'll take a quick look at what makes AngularJS so great.

AN INTUITIVE FRAMEWORK MAKES IT EASY TO ORGANIZE YOUR CODE

As previously stated, there's a pressing need to be able to organize your code in a way that promotes maintenance, collaboration, readability, and extension. AngularJS is constructed in such a way that code has an intuitive place to live, with clear paths to refactor code when it has reached a tipping point. Do you have code that needs to provide information on how a user interface is supposed to look and behave? There's a place for that. Do you have code that needs to contain a portion of your domain model and be available for the rest of the application to use? There's a place for that. Do you need to programmatically perform DOM manipulation? There's even a sane place for that as well!

TESTABLE CODE MAKES IT EASIER TO SLEEP AT NIGHT

Testable code isn't going to win any awards for being the most exciting feature of a framework, but it's the unsung hero of any mature framework. AngularJS was written from the ground up to be testable, and likely this feature, along with the design decisions that came from this commitment, has played a huge role in the adoption of AngularJS. How do you actually know if your application works? The fact that it hasn't broken yet is a flimsy answer, as it's only a matter of time before that black swan shows up at your door.

You can never entirely mitigate against bugs, but you can truly eliminate certain possibilities through rigorous testing. A framework that is conducive to writing testable code is a framework that you're going to write tests in. And when you write tests, you'll spend less time looking over your shoulder wondering when everything is going to come crashing down. You'll be able to go to bed at night and not have to worry about a 2 a.m. call from DevOps that something has gone awry and you need to fix it immediately.

TWO-WAY DATA BINDING SAVES YOU HUNDREDS OF LINES OF CODE

Two-way data binding is the supermodel of the feature set. Hundreds of years ago, when we were writing jQuery applications, you would've had to use jQuery to query the DOM to find a specific element, listen for an event, parse the value of the DOM element, and then perform some action on that value. In AngularJS, you simply have to define a JavaScript property and then bind to it in our HTML, and you're done. There are obviously some variations to this scenario, but it's not uncommon to hear of jQuery applications being rewritten and thousands of lines of JavaScript just disappearing.

By cutting out all of the boilerplate code that was previously required to keep our HTML and JavaScript in sync, you're able to accomplish more work in less time with significantly less effort. This gives you more time to do more of what you love.

TEMPLATES THAT ARE HTML MEANS YOU ALREADY KNOW HOW TO WRITE THEM

HTML is an inherently limited language that was designed to facilitate layout and structure, not complex interactions. In other words, it wasn't created to live in the world of the modern web application as we know it now. Some frameworks try to overcome this limitation by abstracting out HTML entirely into strings or some preprocessor dialect. The problem is that HTML is actually good as a declarative mechanism and there's this annoying reality about HTML—pretty much everyone knows it.

If you're working on a large team, there's a good chance that you're going to have a UI/UX contributor who'll be responsible for generating your HTML templates. It's important to leverage a workflow and skill set that they're already familiar with, and AngularJS makes this a breeze. AngularJS embraces HTML while giving developers the ability to overcome its limitations by extending it to do whatever it is we need.

DATA STRUCTURES THAT ARE JUST JAVASCRIPT MAKE INTEGRATION REALLY EASY

On the flip side, being able to work with Plain Old JavaScript Objects (POJOs) makes integrating with other technologies incredibly easy. By consuming and emitting JavaScript without having to wrap and unwrap it in proprietary framework mechanisms, you're able to consume data from other sources much more efficiently.

You can render JSON models from the server and instantly consume them in AngularJS when the application bootstraps. You can also take the model that you're working with and pass it off to another technology—such as an application server—without having to transform it at all.

There are some pretty interesting features of AngularJS that are fairly academic in nature; we've tried to outline a few major points of how AngularJS makes our lives easier in a very practical sense. At the end of the day, having a framework that allows us to write stable code quickly and efficiently so that we have more time and energy to do other meaningful things is a tool that we want to use!

1.2 The AngularJS big picture

We'll introduce AngularJS from a 10,000-foot view and lay the foundation for what we'll reinforce throughout the entire book (see table 1.1). If you reach the end of the book and you have a solid grasp of figure 1.1 and how all the pieces fit together, we'll have succeeded as authors. If you've absorbed these concepts in such a way that these pieces form a vocabulary in which you start to articulate and express ways to solve your own problems, then we'll have succeeded in a spectacular way!

Table 1.1   AngularJS at a glance

Component	Purpose
Module	Modules serve as containers to help you organize code within your AngularJS application. Modules can contain sub-modules, making it easy to compose functionality as needed.
Config	The config block of an AngularJS application allows for configuration to be applied before the application actually runs. This is useful for setting up routes, dynamically configuring services, and so on.
Routes	Routes allow you to define ways to navigate to specific states within your application. They also allow you to define configuration options for each specific route, such as which template and controller to use.
Views	The view in AngularJS is what exists after AngularJS has compiled and rendered the DOM with all of the JavaScript wiring in place.
$scope	$scope is essentially the glue between the view and controller within an AngularJS application. With the introduction of the *controller-as* syntax, the need to explicitly use $scope has been greatly reduced.
Controller	The controller is responsible for defining methods and properties that the view can bind to and interact with. As a matter of best practice, controllers should be lightweight and only focus on the view they're controlling.
Directive	A directive is an extension of a view in AngularJS in that it allows you to create custom, reusable elements that encapsulate behavior. You can think of directives as components or decorators for your HTML. Directives are used to extend views and to make these extensions available for use in more than one place.
Service	Services provide common functionality to an AngularJS application. For instance, if you have data that more than one controller needs, you would promote that data to a service and then make it available to the controllers via the service. Services extend controllers and make them more globally accessible.

Although we'll get into each of these AngularJS mechanisms in considerable depth in the following chapters, we wanted to introduce you to the major players at the outset so you would have a foundation to build on.

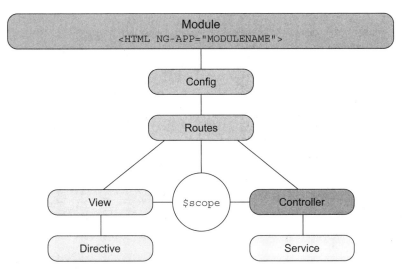

Figure 1.1 The AngularJS big picture

1.3 *Build your first AngularJS application*

Now that you have the AngularJS game pieces on the table, how do you actually use them to put together something useful? This is the perfect time to build something easy with AngularJS. You'll get your feet wet by building a scaled-down version of the sample application for the book; and, in the process, you'll see how these AngularJS pieces fit together without getting too advanced. True to the title of this book, you'll learn AngularJS by seeing it in action and assembling examples that tie into a larger, fully functional application.

The sample application for the book is called Angello; it's a Trello clone that's used to manage user stories. What do we mean by a Trello clone? Well, as some of you may know, Trello is a project management tool that is web-based and founded on a technique that was originally popularized by the Japanese car manufacturer Toyota in the 1980s. Units of work in a project are represented by items—stories, if you will— that can be moved to different positions on a board corresponding to each story's state of progress. The board itself represents the project. We'll properly introduce Angello in the next chapter, but you can see the main screen of Angello in figure 1.2 and the lite version of Angello in figure 1.3. The completed source code for Angello Lite can be found at https://github.com/angularjs-in-action/angello-lite. Download the latest version to your local machine by following the instructions in the README.md on that page.

Over the course of the book, we'll be building out Angello, which you can see in figure 1.2. In the left portion of the screen, the items of work are represented by the white boxes named First Story and Second Story, and the flow of progress is represented by the columns To Do, In Progress, Code Review, QA Review, and Verified, moving from left to right across the screen. As work progresses, each box is moved by

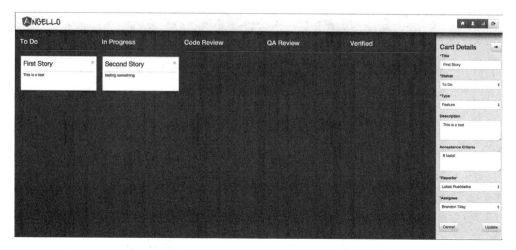

Figure 1.2   Angello

drag-and-drop to represent its state of completion within the project. The details of each work item, each story, can be viewed on the right of the screen. As you may have guessed, each story in Angello represents a unit of computer software that can pass from inception to completion as the project unfolds.

We'll start out by building a simplified version, which you can see in figure 1.3.

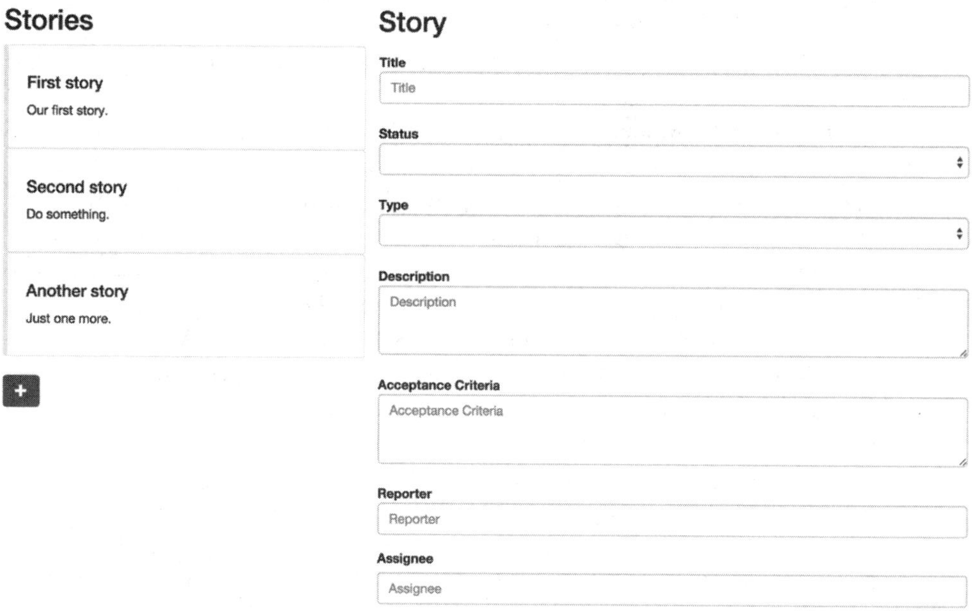

Figure 1.3   Angello Lite

ANGELLO LITE   Because you're pulling files from a CDN, you'll need to run Angello Lite from a web server. There are a few ways to do this, but one of the easiest ways is to use the npm package `serve`.

The steps for installing Angello Lite are as follows:

- Install Node.js. You can find all of the information to do that at http://nodejs.org/.
- Install the serve package by running `npm install -g serve` from the command line.
- Download Angello Lite from GitHub, using the URL given above, and place it on your local machine in a directory named angello-lite.
- Navigate to the angello-lite directory from the command line and run `serve`.
- Go to http://localhost:3000 in your browser to see the application.

Angello Lite is a simplified version of the Angello app that we'll develop from chapter 2 onwards. All the data you add here will be stored in memory alone and not persisted, so when you reload the page, it will be lost. To display the details of an existing story, click the box showing its title and description on the left of the screen. Its details will appear on the right. Use these text boxes and drop-down lists to alter or augment the story and these updates will remain for as long as the page is loaded in the browser. To create a new story, click the plus sign on the left. A new title and description box will appear. Place a new title and description, along with other data, into the text boxes on the right and see how the title and description in the summary box change in real time as you type.

As a high-level overview, figure 1.4 shows the pieces that we'll be building out as they relate to the big picture. We'll start by constructing the module and then build

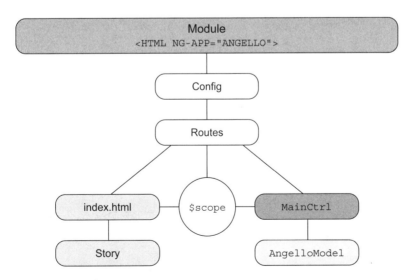

Figure 1.4   Angello and the big picture

out the view and controller via index.html and MainCtrl, respectively. From there we'll introduce services by creating AngelloModel and a directive by creating the story directive.

We won't go through Angello Lite line by line, but we'll sufficiently cover the highlights so that you'll be conversant in what's happening. By the time you finish this chapter, you'll at least be able to fake your way through an AngularJS dinner party!

The thing to keep in mind when building out Angello Lite is that it is a master-detail interface, which shows up in almost every single web application in one form or another. Understanding how to put together a master-detail interface is one of the best foundations for learning how to build web applications in general.

1.3.1 *The module*

Modules in AngularJS serve as containers to help you organize your application into logical units. Modules tell AngularJS how an application is configured and how it's supposed to behave. You can see how it fits into the big picture in figure 1.5.

In our code, we'll create a module called Angello and assign it to the myModule variable:

```
// app.js
var myModule = angular.module('Angello', []);
```

The second parameter is an array that accepts other sub-modules to provide additional functionality, if necessary. It's considered best practice to divide features into sub-modules and then inject them into the main application module. This makes it much easier to move a module around as well as test it.

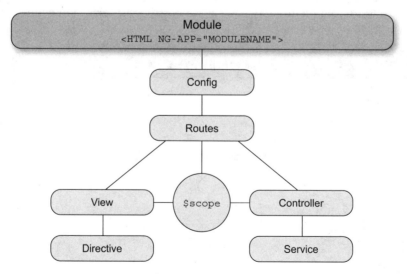

Figure 1.5   The module

You can now define the necessary components for Angello Lite on the `myModule` property. For instance, here we define two services called `AngelloHelper` and `Angello-Model`, as well as a controller called `MainCtrl` and a directive called `story`:

```
// app.js
var myModule = angular.module('Angello', []);
myModule.factory('AngelloHelper', function() { });
myModule.service('AngelloModel', function() { });
myModule.controller('MainCtrl', function() { });
myModule.directive('story', function() { });
```

With the Angello module defined and all of the necessary pieces stubbed out, you can now bootstrap your AngularJS application, using Angello as a starting point. The easiest way to bootstrap an AngularJS application is to add the `ng-app` attribute to the HTML element where you want the AngularJS application to reside. In our case, we want our application to use the entire page, so we'll add `ng-app="Angello"` to the `html` tag. This will bootstrap AngularJS with the `Angello` module:

```
<!-- index.html -->
<html ng-app="Angello">
```

From here, we'll flesh out the remaining pieces with commentary on how they work.

1.3.2 *Views and controllers*

One of the most critical concepts to understand when learning AngularJS is the separation of state from the DOM. AngularJS is officially a Model-View-Whatever (MVW) framework—"Whatever" being whatever pattern helps you be most productive. For the sake of conversation, let's assume that AngularJS follows the Model-View-View-Model (MVVM) design pattern, as established in figure 1.6.

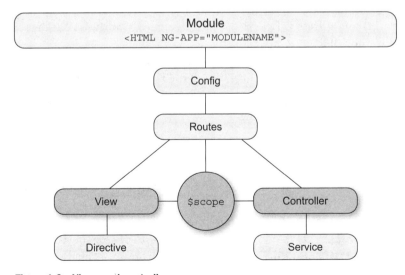

Figure 1.6   Views and controllers

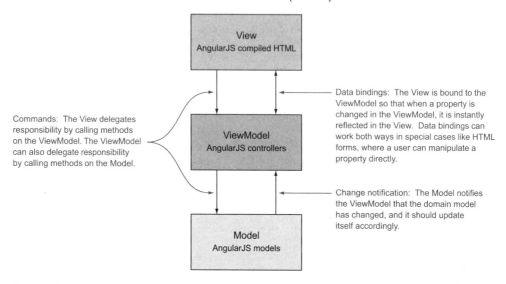

Figure 1.7   Model-View-ViewModel

We'll get to the Model portion in the services section; but for now let's focus on the View and ViewModel parts of this pattern. The View in the MVVM pattern is the view in AngularJS (naturally), and the controller plays the part of the ViewModel, as you can see in figure 1.7.

The controller is responsible for providing state for the view to bind to and commands that the view can issue back to the controller to do units of work. This frees up the view from having to maintain state (since it only has to display whatever state the controller is in) and it frees up the view from having to do any work (as the view always defers to the controller).

To illustrate this in action, we'll first instantiate the `MainCtrl` by adding it to the DOM with the `ng-controller` directive. We use the controller-as syntax by declaring the controller to be `MainCtrl as main`, which means that we'll reference the `MainCtrl` as `main` within the HTML file going forward:

```
<!--index.html-->
<div ng-controller="MainCtrl as main">
</div>
```

Making a property available for binding within the view is just a matter of declaring it on the controller. For instance, you could declare a property on `MainCtrl` such as `this.title` and then immediately bind to it in the view using double curly braces like this: `<h1>{{main.title}}</h1>`. Any changes to the `title` property would instantly be reflected in the DOM. Binding to a simple string property is fairly simplistic, so let's do something more in-depth and bind to an actual collection. We'll create an array containing multiple `story` objects and define it as `stories` on `MainCtrl`:

```
// app.js
myModule.controller('MainCtrl', function() {
    var main = this;

    //...
    main.stories = [
        {
            title: 'First story',
            description: 'Our first story.',
            criteria: 'Criteria pending.',
            status: 'To Do',
            type: 'Feature',
            reporter: 'Lukas Ruebbelke',
            assignee: 'Brian Ford'
        },
        {
            title: 'Second story',
            description: 'Do something.',
            criteria: 'Criteria pending.',
            status: 'Back Log',
            type: 'Feature',
            reporter: 'Lukas Ruebbelke',
            assignee: 'Brian Ford'
        },
        {
            title: 'Another story',
            description: 'Just one more.',
            criteria: 'Criteria pending.',
            status: 'Code Review',
            type: 'Enhancement',
            reporter: 'Lukas Ruebbelke',
            assignee: 'Brian Ford'
        }
    ];
    //...
});
```

THIS Per common convention, we like to store a reference to the top-level `this` object in case we need it later; `this` has a habit of changing context based on function level scope. We also like to name the reference to `this` the same name we declare the *controller-as* in the view—as in `main` for `MainCtrl as main`. This makes it easier to read and connect the dots as you jump between the HTML and the JavaScript.

We'll display the `main.stories` collection as a list of items that comprise the master portion of the master-detail view. The first thing we need to do is to repeat over the `main.stories` array and create an individual display element for each story item in the array. The `ng-repeat` directive accomplishes this by going through every item in the `main.stories` collection and creating a copy of the HTML element it was declared on and all of its child elements. So by declaring `ng-repeat="story in main.stories"` on our callout div, we're essentially telling AngularJS to loop through `main.stories` and reference each individual item as `story`—which we can bind to within the child elements:

```
<!-- index.html -->
<div ng-controller="MainCtrl as main">
    <div class="col-md-4">
        <h2>Stories</h2>
        <div class="callout"
             ng-repeat="story in main.stories"
             ng-click="main.setCurrentStory(story)">
        <h4>{{story.title}}</h4>
        <p>{{story.description}}</p>
        </div>
    </div>
</div>
```

Each `story` object has a title and description property, which we can bind to via `{{story.title}}` and `{{story.description}}`. AngularJS is really good at providing context within each template instance, so we don't have to worry about the `story` instance getting overwritten with each iteration. This is important when we want to start doing things like `ng-click="main.setCurrentStory(story)"`, in which the specific instance of `story` matters a great deal.

This is a perfect segue for moving beyond binding to properties and learning how to bind to expressions. You can also make methods available to the view by declaring them on the controller. For instance, we'll define a method called `main.createStory` that pushes a new `story` object into the `main.stories` array:

```
// app.js
myModule.controller('MainCtrl', function() {
    var main = this;

    //...
    main.createStory = function() {
        main.stories.push({
            title:'New Story',
            description:'Description pending.',
            criteria:'Criteria pending.',
            status:'Back Log',
            type:'Feature',
            reporter:'Pending',
            assignee:'Pending'
        });
    };
    //...
});
```

Now that `createStory` is defined on the `MainCtrl`, it's available to be called from the view. We can then call `main.createStory` from the view by using `ng-click` on an anchor tag:

```
<!-- index.html -->
<div ng-controller="MainCtrl as main">
    <div class="col-md-4">
        <h2>Stories</h2>
        <div class="callout"
             ng-repeat="story in main.stories"
             ng-click="main.setCurrentStory(story)">
```

```
            <h4>{{story.title}}</h4>
            <p>{{story.description}}</p>
        </div>
        <br/>
        <a class="btn btn-primary" ng-click="main.createStory()">
            <span class="glyphicon glyphicon-plus"></span>
        </a>
    </div>
</div>
```

Using a ViewModel inverts the application flow that traditionally existed in jQuery-style applications. In jQuery, you would've queried the DOM and attached an event listener. When that event fired, you would try to interpret the event and parse the DOM for state so that you could perform some imperative operation. This forces a tight coupling between the HTML and the JavaScript that drives it. By introducing a ViewModel, you're able to break this relationship. The controller no longer is responsible for listening to the view, but rather the view is responsible for issuing specific commands to the controller that it operates on.

> **MVVM** A full-fledged discussion on the MVVM pattern is outside the scope of this book, but we recommend reading up on it here: http://en.wikipedia.org/wiki/Model_View_ViewModel. Having a clear separation between declarative markup and imperative logic is conducive to better, more stable code that is easier to test.

1.3.3 Services

If controllers should be lightweight and specific to the view for which they're responsible, what happens if two controllers need to share the same information? Controllers definitely shouldn't know about each other. So what happens if some piece of information starts in one controller and you realize that it needs to be available in another controller? The answer to these questions is an AngularJS *service*. You promote (extract) the common data from the controller and make it available to the entire application by exposing it via a service. As you can see in figure 1.8, this is the Model portion of the Model-View-ViewModel pattern.

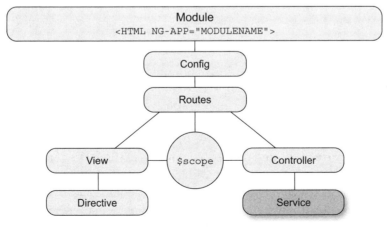

Figure 1.8 Services

In the previous section, we populated our `stories` collection directly in the `MainCtrl`, but now we'll promote that collection to the `AngelloModel` service and make it available to the `MainCtrl`. We'll declare a `stories` property in `AngelloModel` and then populate it with the same collection we used in `MainCtrl`:

```
// app.js
myModule.service('AngelloModel', function() {
    var service = this,
        stories = [
            {
                title: 'First story',
                description: 'Our first story.',
                criteria: 'Criteria pending.',
                status: 'To Do',
                type: 'Feature',
                reporter: 'Lukas Ruebbelke',
                assignee: 'Brian Ford'
            },
            //...
        ];

    service.getStories = function() {
        return stories;
    };
});
```

From here, we'll make `AngelloModel` available to `MainCtrl` by passing it into the constructor function as a parameter. AngularJS uses *dependency injection* (DI) to provide dependencies where they're needed. Dependency injection is fancier in name than it is in implementation. AngularJS can detect that we need an instance of `AngelloModel`, so it creates an instance for use and injects it into `MainCtrl`, thus fulfilling that dependency:

```
// app.js
myModule.controller('MainCtrl', function(AngelloModel) {
    var main = this;

    //...
    main.stories = AngelloModel.getStories();
    //...
});
```

We can now populate `main.stories` by assigning to it the return value of `AngelloModel.getStories()`. The beauty of this arrangement is that `MainCtrl` is completely oblivious to where the stories data is coming from or how we got it. We'll get into this in much greater depth in the following chapters, but we could've just as easily made a remote server call and populated the data that way.

One more quick example, and then we'll move on to directives. AngularJS services aren't just for storing common state, but also for sharing common functionality, such as utility functions. For example, we needed a very general `buildIndex` method to take an array and create an index based on a property parameter. That way we wouldn't have to loop over the array every single time we needed to find an object in it. This type of a general function could be used in more than one place, so we put it in an AngelloHelper service:

```
// app.js
myModule.factory('AngelloHelper', function() {
    var buildIndex = function(source, property) {
        var tempArray = [];

        for(var i = 0, len = source.length; i < len; ++i) {
            tempArray[source[i][property]] = source[i];
        }

        return tempArray;
    };

    return {
        buildIndex: buildIndex
    };
});
```

This kind of finely grained code is much easier to maintain and test because it is in isolation and doesn't depend on some other runtime context.

1.3.4 Directives

Directives are one of the most powerful and exciting things in AngularJS. In fact, you've already seen some directives in action in the previous sections. For instance, when you attach ng-click to an element, you're using a built-in AngularJS directive to augment the behavior of that specific element. When you add ng-app or ng-controller to the page, you're using AngularJS directives to provide new behavior to an otherwise static page. In figure 1.9, you can see how they fit into the big picture.

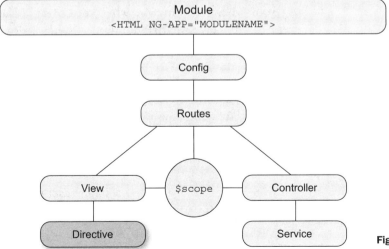

Figure 1.9 Directives

We'll introduce a simple directive to Angello Lite to get our feet wet. We'll create a story directive that represents a story in the page. Directives are defined similarly to controllers and services in that they take a name and a function defining their behavior:

```
// app.js
myModule.directive('story', function(){
    return {
        scope: true,
        replace: true,
        template:'<div><h4>{{story.title}}</h4>
        ➥ <p>{{story.description}}</p></div>'
    }
});
```

The function returns a *directive definition object* (DDO) that defines how the directive is supposed to be configured. We're telling AngularJS that each instance of this directive gets a new scope and that the template we defined replaces the element the directive was defined on. The template markup should be familiar, as it's the same code we used previously to display the title and description of the current story item.

Now that we've defined the directive, we update the HTML in our page to use a story tag and not a div tag. A story tag? Is there even such a thing? There is now!

```
<div ng-controller="MainCtrl as main">
    <div class="col-md-4">
        <h2>Stories</h2>
        <story class="callout"
                ng-repeat="story in main.stories"
                ng-click="main.setCurrentStory(story)">
        </story>
        <!-- ... -->
    </div>
</div>
```

Even though this is a small example of how to extend HTML to do new things by using directives, we want to start your wheels turning on what kind of applications you would write if you could create HTML tags and attributes to do whatever you wanted.

1.4   Summary

This concludes our tour of Angello Lite. Now that you've seen most of the major players from figure 1.1 in action, we'll spend the rest of the book digging into these concepts a lot deeper and in a more useful context as we start to work with Angello.

Let's do a quick review before we finish this chapter and head into the next one:

- AngularJS was created as a framework designed to make it easier to write and organize large JavaScript applications.
- AngularJS was written from the ground up to be testable; as a result, it's much easier to write clean, stable code that can scale.

- Data binding saves you from writing literally thousands—if not tens of thousands—of lines of code because you no longer have to write tedious boilerplate around DOM events.
- Because AngularJS templates are just HTML, it's easy to leverage existing skill sets to build out UIs in AngularJS.
- Plain Old JavaScript Objects make integration with other systems much easier.
- AngularJS modules are containers for organizing your application.
- Views in AngularJS are compiled and rendered HTML with a controller attached.
- A controller is the ViewModel for the view and is responsible for providing data and methods for the view to bind to.
- Services encapsulate and provide common functionality in an AngularJS application.
- A directive is a custom component or attribute that extends HTML to do new and powerful things.

Structuring your
AngularJS application

This chapter covers

- Introduction to Angello
- How to structure an AngularJS project so it can scale
- Introducing basic routes and navigation
- Building the basic structure for starting a web application
- Some basic best practices for developing AngularJS applications

2.1   Hello Angello

In the previous chapter, using a limited example, you saw how the major pieces of AngularJS fit together to build web applications. Though Angello Lite is a great place to get acquainted with AngularJS, it's our desire to show you how a non-trivial AngularJS application fits together in the real world. To that end, we'd like to introduce you to the official sample application of the book—Angello.

WHY ANGELLO? One of the first really impressive web applications that we remember seeing was Trello, and it has always had a special place in our hearts. Just as a reminder, Trello is a web application that allows you to organize lists within lists and claims to have "everything you need to organize projects of any size." That's why we wanted to use Trello as the inspiration for building out an AngularJS version of Trello for the book, for organizing coding projects. That's also why it's fondly called Angello.

The source code for Angello can be found on GitHub at the repository https://github.com/angularjs-in-action/angello, and you can also check out a live version of Angello at http://www.angelloinaction.com/.

A lot of thought has gone into the process of adequately covering server-side communication while staying focused on AngularJS and minimizing the cognitive overhead that comes with spinning up a development server. At the time of this writing, there are two fairly painless options for running a back-end server.

The first and easiest option is to use Firebase as the back end. This can be set up and integrated in just a few minutes from a totally free account. The second option is to use the Node.js API that's at the *AngularJS in Action* GitHub site. We recommend trying both because they provide equally valuable learning opportunities. Check the appendixes for detailed instructions on how to set up the back end of your choosing.

There are four main sections to Angello: the login screen, the home or storyboard screen, the user screen, and the dashboard screen.

The login screen (see figure 2.1) is where users authenticate before they can navigate anywhere else in the application. This will be the splash screen if you're a logged-out

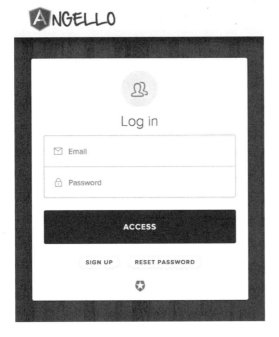

Figure 2.1 The Angello login screen

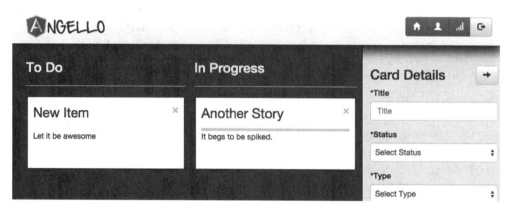

Figure 2.2   The Angello home screen

user. To use Angello, you must create a username. If you haven't already, fill out the Log In form and click Sign Up.

The home screen (see figure 2.2) is where most of the interaction within Angello takes place. Users can create and manage user stories, visualizing them as cards divided into *swimlanes*. You work on these user stories by creating software that will go through a process of testing and validation and final acceptance; the cards representing these units of work will be positioned on the screen in a way that reflects this process.

The user screen (see figure 2.3) is where new users can be added or existing users can be updated. There's also a secondary screen (which we'll cover in the routing chapter) that allows you to see all the stories assigned to that user.

The dashboard screen (see figure 2.4) allows you to visualize user stories by status and type in graph form. We'll cover how this happens in chapter 5.

The goal with Angello is to cover as many common development tasks as possible with code and techniques that can be quickly modified to suit your needs. We'll use

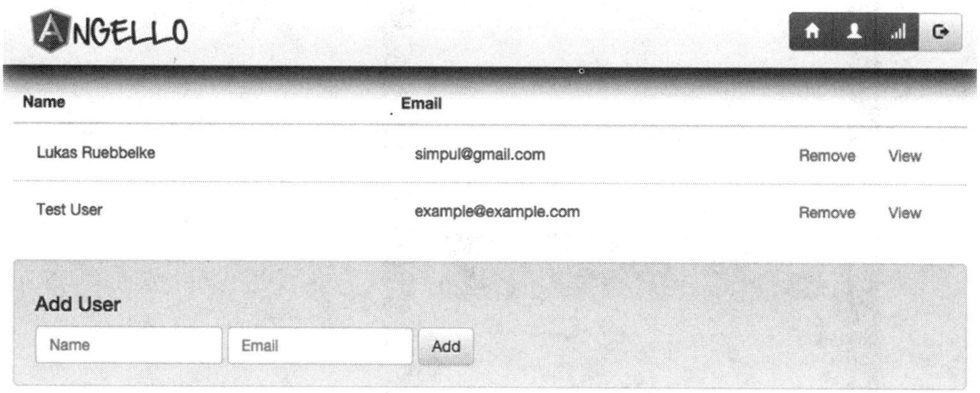

Figure 2.3   The Angello user screen

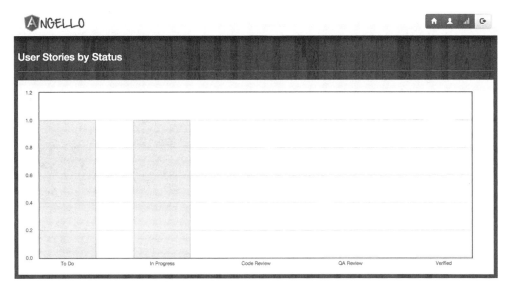

Figure 2.4　The Angello dashboard

Angello as a context, but try to think of ways that you can apply the things you're learning to the work you're doing right now.

2.2　*AngularJS application structure*

With that in mind, the first thing that warrants a discussion when building web applications is this: how does someone actually structure their application so that they don't live to regret it as complexity increases? The interesting thing about a good file structure is that it has almost the same requirements as good code. In fact, it's not uncommon to see a distinct parallel between the file structure and code organization of an application.

File structure

A good file structure makes it easy to navigate, maintain, and extend. It's also important that the file structure be self-documenting and clearly indicate intention. Someone should be able to look at the file structure and quickly have a high-level understanding of what elements make up the app and what the app does.

CLEAN CODE　One our favorite programming books is *Clean Code: A Handbook of Agile Software Craftsmanship* by Robert C. Martin (2009, Pearson Education). We recommend that everyone read it. Once a year.

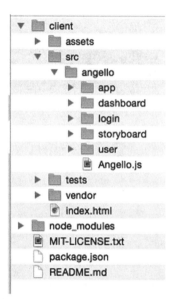

Figure 2.5   The Angello file structure

Remember the four main Angello features that we discussed earlier? Look at figure 2.5 and see if you notice anything interesting.

In the angello folder, there's a folder for each of the features in Angello. There's also an app folder that contains all of the common functionality that needs to be shared across all of the specific features.

There are two common approaches to structuring an AngularJS application—by type or by feature. For example, if you were to organize your files by type, you'd put all your controllers in a folder, all your services in a folder, and so forth. If you're organizing by feature, you'll put all of the files that support a single feature in that directory. A hybrid approach has also emerged that we tend to favor—to organize file structure by feature and then, within feature, organize by type. This allows for a

Figure 2.6   A deeper look at the file structure

modular design but makes it easier for new developers to get up to speed quickly on a project. If you're using Grunt or Gulp, this becomes less of an implementation detail—all of your source files are concatenated in the distribution build anyway. See figure 2.6.

DO WHAT'S RIGHT FOR YOU Best practices have a way of becoming religious topics, and we encourage everyone to avoid that entirely. We believe we should favor a convention that helps us build things better and faster. Choose a solution that works best for you and your team and stick with it. Consistency is more important than being "right."

2.3   *Laying the Angello foundation*

The first topic we'll cover in starting to build out Angello is how the AngularJS modules fit together. Modules are the building blocks of your application, and understanding how these fit together will make adding new functionality in the future easier. In fact, we often visualize our applications from a high level by their module structure.

In every AngularJS application, there will be a single, top-level module that will serve as the initialization point for every other module in the application. Generally, this top-level module will do little other than connect the appropriate sub-modules and apply some application-wide configuration settings. In Angello, our top-level module is appropriately called `Angello`. We'll use it to bootstrap our application in the index.html file via `ng-app="Angello"`:

```
<!-- client/index.html -->
<html ng-app="Angello">
    <!-- HTML -->
```

In our Angello.js file, we'll create the Angello module and declare its sub-module dependencies. Because we're using AngularJS routing and animations, we're going to inject the `ngRoute` and `ngAnimate` sub-modules. As mentioned before, we're offering two options for handling back-end communication and authentication: Firebase and Node.js. To enable them, we need to inject the `firebase`, `auth0`, `angular-jwt`, and `angular-storage` sub-modules. Last but not least, we'll use the sub-module `ngMessages` for form validation:

```
// client/src/angello/Angello.js
var myModule = angular.module('Angello',
    [
        'ngRoute',
        'ngAnimate',
        'firebase',
        'ngMessages',
        'Angello.Common',
        'Angello.Dashboard',
        'Angello.Login',
        'Angello.Storyboard',
        'Angello.User',
        'auth0',
        'angular-jwt',
        'angular-storage'
    ]);
```

We also have a sub-module for every feature of Angello, including one for the common functionality that's shared between the features. This allows us to look at how the

Angello module is being constructed and quickly establish a mental picture of the pieces that make up the application. It would appear that Angello is actually serving as a platform on which we're attaching a bunch of smaller, more specific applications; that's by design.

You've seen how the top-level module is configured, but what about a sub-module? Let's examine the Angello.Storyboard module to see how it's constructed. It's constructed using the same angular.module method call that takes the name of the new module as a string and an array of its dependencies:

```
// client/src/angello/storyboard/Storyboard.js
angular.module('Angello.Storyboard', ['Angello.Common']);
```

The Angello.Storyboard module needs to have access to the user stories, but so do all of the other modules, which is why the StoriesModel is part of Angello.Common. Generally speaking, models will go into the common module so that they can be shared across the entire application. Once we've injected Angello.Common into the Angello.Storyboard module, we can now make calls to the StoriesModel, as you can see in the StoryboardCtrl:

```
// client/src/angello/storyboard/controllers/StoryboardController.js
angular.module('Angello.Storyboard')
    .controller('StoryboardCtrl',
        function () {
        //...
    });
```

You can see in the following code that StoriesModel is being declared on Angello.Common:

```
// client/src/angello/app/models/StoriesModel.js
angular.module('Angello.Common')
    .service('StoriesModel',
        function () {
            //...
        });
```

> **PLEASE BE CAREFUL** To get an AngularJS module, you'll call angular.module without the second parameter. We've unfortunately run into some unpredictable behavior by accidentally putting in an empty array as the second parameter, which will overwrite the module definition and create a new one. It's easy to make this mistake when you're tired.

2.4 *Basic routes and navigation*

With the modules in place, the next step is to set up the ability to navigate from one feature to another. We'll start out with ngRoute, since it's incredibly simple (albeit limited) to implement within an application.

> **DON'T WANT TO KEEP IT SIMPLE?** We're only covering ngRoute in the book, but we recommend looking into ui-router also, because it's a powerful, full-featured router. You can read about it here: https://github.com/angular-ui/ui-router.

Routes allow you to define and route to a unique state of the application based on the current URL. For instance, if we wanted to link a colleague directly to the users section of the application, we could send them a link such as http://angelloinaction.com/#/users and expect that Angello would be able to route our colleague to that portion of the application.

Using the Angello header as our reference point (see figure 2.7), we'll define a route for each navigation item. We'll start by defining a route for the root of the site, which is denoted with a forward slash. Because the storyboard is the most important feature of the application, we'll make this the feature at the root of the site.

Figure 2.7   The Angello header

The module class in AngularJS comes with a handful of convenience methods that make configuring our application a lot easier. The `module.config` method is a convenient method for defining configuration options before the application has actually run. Routes are exactly the kind of thing that we want in place before the application is exposed to the user.

In our main application file, we'll call `myModule.config` and pass in the `$routeProvider` service, which is responsible for configuring routes. Routes are configured by calling `$routeProvider.when` and passing in a route (a.k.a. URL string) and a configuration object for that particular route. The route configuration object can vary in complexity, but in its simplest form, it's responsible for associating a template and a controller to a particular route.

```
// client/src/angello/Angello.js
myModule.config(function($routeProvider) {
    $routeProvider
        .when('/', {
            templateUrl: 'src/angello/storyboard/tmpl/storyboard.html',
            controller: 'StoryboardCtrl',
            controllerAs: 'storyboard'
        });
});
```

We accomplish this by defining the `templateUrl` property to point to the story-board.html template and the controller property to reference the `StoryboardCtrl`. Because we're using the *controller-as* syntax, we'll add the `controllerAs` property and give it a value of `storyboard`.

Now that we've defined a route, how does it actually make it on the page? Routing with `ngRoute` is generally used in tandem with the `ng-view` directive. When a route is matched with the `$routeProvider`, it will look for the `ng-view` directive and then load and compile the template into it. In the following simplified version of the `index.html` page, when the page is loaded for the first time, the `$routeProvider` will detect that we're at the root of the application and load the storyboard.html template into the div with `ng-view=""` declared on it. Prior to loading the template, it will be compiled with `StoryboardCtrl` so that all of the bindings are in place and render properly. Note that in the Angello application proper, a URL request for the root of the application will bring up the login screen if the user isn't currently logged in.

```
<!-- client/index.html -->
<html ng-app="Angello">
    <head></head>
    <body ng-controller="MainCtrl as main">
        <div class="navbar navbar-fixed-top navbar-default"></div>
        <div ng-view=""></div>
        <div class="modal"></div>
    </body>
</html>
```

NGROUTE LIMITATION   You're only allowed to declare one `ng-view` on your page; this is one of the most glaring shortcomings of `ngRoute`.

With a root route defined for the root of the application, we'll set up the logo to return us to the root of the site:

```
<!-- client/index.html -->
<div class="navbar navbar-fixed-top navbar-default">
    <div class="navbar-header">
        <a class="logo navbar-brand" href="#/">
            <img src="assets/img/angello.png">
        </a>
    </div>
</div>
<!-- ... -->
```

We'll wrap the logo in an anchor tag and set the `href` to navigate to #/. By default, routes work with a hashtag, but you can set it to HTML5 mode to not use the hashtag or override the default delimiter if you wish. Because you have to turn some dials at the server to make HTML5 mode work properly, we'll go with the default implementation.

So we know that the `$routeProvider` matches the URL to a route and then orchestrates the template and controller for that route, but what happens if there isn't a route match? We can mitigate the risk of a user finding themselves in the weeds by defining a fallback using the `otherwise` method on `$routeProvider`. In the following code, we tell the application to match a route if it can; otherwise, just redirect to the root of the application:

```
// client/src/angello/Angello.js
myModule.config(function($routeProvider) {
    $routeProvider
        .when('/', {
            templateUrl: 'src/angello/storyboard/tmpl/storyboard.html',
            controller: 'StoryboardCtrl',
            controllerAs: 'storyboard'
        })
        .otherwise({redirectTo: '/'});
});
```

One of the beautiful things with `$routeProvider` is that we can daisy-chain our routes, which makes for a more elegant route table. We've established a pattern for a single route; now check out the entire route table and notice the consistency and convention that exists for all of the routes:

```
// client/src/angello/Angello.js
myModule.config(function($routeProvider) {
    $routeProvider
        .when('/', {
            templateUrl: 'src/angello/storyboard/tmpl/storyboard.html',
            controller: 'StoryboardCtrl',
            controllerAs: 'storyboard'
        })
        .when('/dashboard', {
            templateUrl: 'src/angello/dashboard/tmpl/dashboard.html',
            controller: 'DashboardCtrl',
            controllerAs: 'dashboard'
        })
        .when('/users', {
            templateUrl: 'src/angello/user/tmpl/users.html',
            controller: 'UsersCtrl',
            controllerAs: 'users'
        })
        .when('/users/:userId', {
            templateUrl: 'src/angello/user/tmpl/user.html',
            controller: 'UserCtrl',
            controllerAs: 'myUser'
        })
        .when('/login', {
            templateUrl: 'src/angello/login/tmpl/login.html',
            controller: 'LoginCtrl',
            controllerAs: 'login'
        })
        .otherwise({redirectTo: '/'});
});
```

And in the navigation bar, we link to the root, users, and dashboard pages via #/, #/users, and #/dashboard, respectively:

```
<!-- client/index.html -->
<div class="navbar navbar-fixed-top navbar-default">
    <div class="navbar-header">
        <a class="logo navbar-brand" href="#/">
            <img src="assets/img/angello.png">
        </a>
    </div>
    <div class="btn-group pull-right" ng-show="main.currentUser">
        <a class="btn btn-danger" href="#/">
            <span class="glyphicon glyphicon-home"></span>
        </a>
        <a class="btn btn-danger" href="#/users">
            <span class="glyphicon glyphicon-user"></span>
        </a>
        <a class="btn btn-danger" href="#/dashboard">
```

```
            <span class="glyphicon glyphicon-signal"></span>
        </a>
        <!-- ... -->
    </div>
</div>
```

We could have used `ng-click` and the `$location` service to change the route, but it's considered best practice to use anchor tags where possible to stay consistent with how a user expects the browser to work. Manually changing routes with JavaScript breaks things, for example, the ability to click and open in a new tab.

2.5   *A few best practices*

We'll take a moment to cover a few principles that are important for writing an AngularJS application that can evolve in terms of features and complexity.

Controllers should be lightweight and specific to the view they control. A controller should be solely concerned with consuming data, preparing it for the view, and transmitting data to services for processing.

Controllers should be oblivious to the world around them unless you specifically tell them about it. In other words, a controller shouldn't know about the view it controls and should definitely not know about other controllers.

Services should hold your domain model and do all of the heavy lifting, including server-side communication.

Keep your declarative markup outside of your controllers; conversely, keep your imperative logic outside of your views. It's really easy to clutter up your view with a complex condition such as `ng-if="thisCondition && anotherCondition && yetAnotherCondition"`. This is hard to maintain and test. Instead, extract that logic structure into a method and bind to that like so: `ng-if="shouldShowThis()"`. This way it is easy to extend `should-ShowThis` and actually possible to test it.

If you must programmatically manipulate the DOM, then do it in a link function in a directive. This is 99.9% true with a few exceptions, such as a modal service.

Keep your methods fine-grained and as functional (pure) as possible to make testing them easier. This is a general programming principle that's worth its weight in gold.

> **STYLE GUIDES**   Todd Motto and John Papa have written excellent style guides that we recommend you check out. These guides are designed to offer helpful suggestions that have worked well for them on large projects; but they suggest you pick what works for you:
>
> - Todd Motto's Style Guide—https://github.com/toddmotto/angularjs-styleguide
> - John Papa's Style Guide—https://github.com/johnpapa/angularjs-styleguide

There are many tips and tricks that we could get into, but these are the fundamental principles that have the most value for developers learning AngularJS. JavaScript can be idiosyncratic, but it hasn't negated the timeless principles that have existed in software development for years.

2.6 *Summary*

In this chapter, we laid the foundation for our sample application by discussing file structure, module composition, and basic routes. We also touched on some best practices that we'll use to guide our project as we continue to develop it throughout the book.

Let's do a quick review before we move on:

- The sample application is called Angello, and it's a Trello clone, built in AngularJS, that manages user stories.
- The file structure for an application should be self-documenting and easy to work with. The best approach for this is to divide your files by feature (and possibly by type within that feature). The goal is to treat each feature as if it were a miniature application unto itself.
- The top-level module is responsible for composing the sub-modules into a working application.
- The file structure and the module composition of an AngularJS application often mirror each other.
- Basic routes can be set up in the `module.config` block using `$routeProvider`.
- A basic route definition involves matching a template and a controller together to be loaded into the `ng-view` directive when `$routeProvider` detects a matching route.

Part 2

Make something
with AngularJS

The next five chapters expand on the project from part 1 as we start to build out a full-fledged version of the sample application, Angello. Angello pays homage to the web application Trello while using it as the backdrop for discussing various AngularJS techniques such as server-side communication, directives, forms and validations, animations, and so on.

In chapter 3, you'll learn how views and controllers work together in AngularJS to control what the user sees, as well as capture user interactions and convey those events for processing. We expand on controllers in chapter 4 by introducing services and then showing how to communicate with a remote server using the `$http service`. In chapter 5 we extend our views by introducing directives and showing how directives turn our layouts into components while providing complex functionality. We'll kick our layout up a notch in chapter 6 by easily adding in animations using `ngAnimate`. In chapter 7, we'll dig into how to use routes in AngularJS to deep-link to specific states in our application by preloading specific data using `resolve` and passing variables from route to route using `$routeParams`. We'll finish things off in chapter 8 with a discussion on how to use form validation to enhance the user experience while providing safeguards around the data being entered.

You can find the source code for the final project here: https://github.com/angularjs-in-action/angello. You can also see a production version of Angello here: http://www.angelloinaction.com/.

Views and controllers

This chapter covers

- What a view is in AngularJS
- Creating controllers to manage views
- Declaring properties and methods in a controller
- Binding to properties and expressions in an AngularJS template
- Best practices for creating views and controllers and how to test them

In this chapter, we'll get into the most fundamental and important facet in AngularJS. You'll learn what views and controllers are in AngularJS, and more importantly the relationship that they have with each other. There may be some edge case that we haven't considered but by our approximation, everything in AngularJS is designed to either support views and controllers, or to extend their functionality.

The goal of this chapter is to build out the storyboard view in Angello, as seen in figure 3.1. This storyboard view will give you plenty of opportunities to learn how a view works in AngularJS and how you can control that view with a controller. You'll learn how to take an array of JavaScript objects and display them as user stories, and

Figure 3.1   The storyboard view

then how to create, update, and delete items in the user story collection by exposing that functionality via the controller.

In Angello, we're binding to an array of story objects in order to display them in the view, but we could just as easily bind to an array of song objects and display a playlist or an array of ingredients to make a recipe. You can literally take any collection of values and display them with an AngularJS template. Using built-in AngularJS directives, you can capture user interactions and then modify the collection by adding, updating, or deleting items within the collection.

3.1   The big picture

Before we get into the specific implementation details of how the storyboard view is constructed, we'll spend a brief moment talking about the relationship between views and controllers, as seen in figure 3.2.

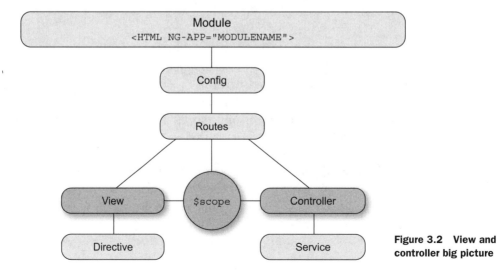

Figure 3.2   View and controller big picture

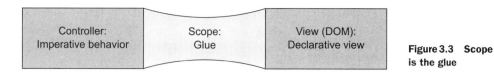

Figure 3.3 Scope is the glue

A *view* in AngularJS is the HTML after it has been compiled by AngularJS, and is the interface that the user sees. At the core, a *controller* is a JavaScript object that contains methods and properties. The view contains the declarative markup and the controller possesses code to define imperative behavior. As it stands, the view and controller are completely separated from each other, with nothing to connect the two. This is where scope comes into the picture (see figure 3.3).

The glue between the view and the controller is *scope*. The controller is responsible for exposing methods and properties to the view by attaching them to scope. When a method or property is declared on scope, it's available to interact with the view. For the sake of convenience, most people generally think of the controller and scope as a single entity that behaves essentially like a ViewModel.

If you examine figure 3.4, you can see how this relationship exists with some simple pseudocode. The form in `user.html` is bound to the `user` object on `$scope` in the `UserController`. When the form changes, `$scope.user` is immediately updated to reflect the changes. The converse is also true when `$scope.user` is updated; the form will also update to reflect the state of the object. When the Save button is clicked, the view issues a command to the controller in the form of a `$scope.save` method call. The controller can also issue commands to services, which you see in the `UserModel.save` method call.

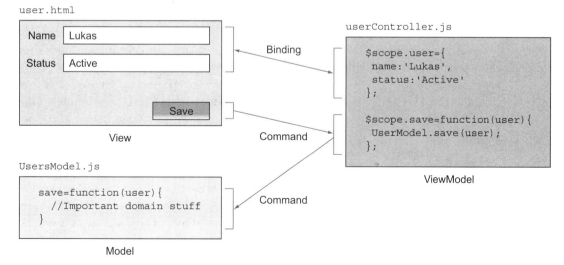

Figure 3.4 MVVM according to AngularJS

We'll get into services and models in the following chapter, but for now let's focus on views and controllers.

3.2   *What is an AngularJS view?*

If you go to the AngularJS home page at https://angularjs.org, you'll see a bold proclamation front and center of what AngularJS is, and that is "HTML enhanced for web apps!" What exactly does that mean? The implications of this statement will continue to unfold as you learn and experiment with AngularJS. At the most rudimentary level, it means that you have a convenient way to bind HTML to JavaScript objects and keep them synchronized while eliminating the boilerplate code that was traditionally necessary to accomplish this. This also means that you have some custom HTML tags and elements, also known as *directives*, that you can use to do some clever things fairly quickly.

Declaring a property on scope such as `$scope.name` and then displaying it in HTML is as simple as `<p>{{name}}</p>`, and this relationship between the HTML and JavaScript is established seamlessly behind the scenes with AngularJS. If you had an array of values such as `$scope.values = [0,1,2,3,4]` and you wanted to display them in the HTML, it would be as simple as `<p ng-repeat="value in values">{{value}}</p>`. AngularJS provides an entire set of custom attributes and elements that allow you to perform operations efficiently and with little ceremony. Learning how to declare bindings and leverage AngularJS directives is exciting, and most people are blown away at how much they are able to accomplish with so little.

The built-in AngularJS directives can't possibly account for every real-world scenario, and so the AngularJS team provided a way to address this by allowing you to write your own custom directives. This is where the relationship with AngularJS expands beyond being just about productivity to encompass expression. It's easy to get excited about writing HTML when you realize that you can literally create any tag or attribute you want to express whatever it is you're trying to accomplish. We'll get into directives in a later chapter, but this discussion brings us back full circle: once you learn to write directives, you'll have a moment of realization where you realize what those funny tags you used when you started with AngularJS actually are, and how they work. AngularJS is essentially using itself to do most of the heavy lifting for you!

With that in mind, what exactly is an AngularJS view? The simplest answer is this: what exists after AngularJS has compiled the DOM. We'll get into what actually happens during the compilation process, but for now let's think of compilation as the act of gluing the HTML and controllers together with scope.

The AngularJS compilation cycle happens in two parts: the compilation phase and the linking phase. When the HTML is fully loaded, AngularJS parses the DOM and compiles a list of all of the AngularJS directives; this is known as the *compilation phase*. Once full inventory has been made of the HTML, AngularJS enters the linking phase, which is responsible for linking the AngularJS pieces to an appropriate scope instance (see figure 3.5).

Once the AngularJS template has been linked with its appropriate controller via scope, the bindings become active and the two can communicate.

The AngularJS compilation cycle

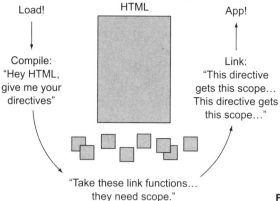

Figure 3.5   HTML meets scope meets HTML

The compilation process is implicit, and the linking between the AngularJS templates and scope is seamless, but you can also manually compile templates and scope together. The need to actually do this is a bit of an edge case, but the function call is surprisingly effective at illustrating what's happening:

```
$compile(element.contents())(scope);
```

In the method call, we're taking the contents of an HTML element and "zipping" it up with a scope object.

3.3   What is an AngularJS controller?

We've established that scope is the glue that binds the view and controller together, but what is it exactly? If you were to throw back the curtain to reveal the wizard that's making all of this happening, you'd simply have a plain old JavaScript object with some events baked into it. These events exist to facilitate a *digest cycle* in AngularJS, which is what keeps the view and controller synchronized (see figure 3.6).

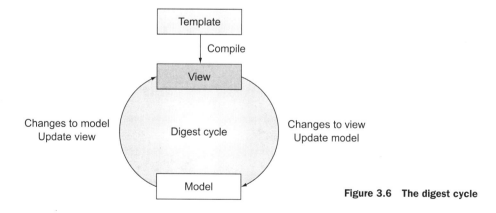

Figure 3.6   The digest cycle

3.3.1   *The digest cycle*

So let's take a moment and answer the burning question: how does AngularJS know when something has changed and it's time to update? It works on a concept of *dirty checking*, and it's one of the core tenets of how the entire framework operates.

Here we need a disclaimer that the next couple of paragraphs slant toward the academic side. AngularJS works just fine without a deep understanding of what's going on at a molecular level. Feel free to skip this section, but for the curious, read on!

Dirty checking is the simple process of comparing a value with its previous value, and if it has changed, then a change event is fired.

AngularJS performs dirty checking via a digest cycle that's controlled by `$digest`. `$digest` happens implicitly, and you never have to call this directly. If you need to initiate a digest cycle, then use `$apply`; it calls `$digest` but has error-handling mechanisms built around it.

During the compilation phase, `$scope` evaluates all of its properties and creates a watch expression for each one. You can manually create watch expressions, but implicitly created watch expressions are simple functions that compare the value of the property with the previous value using `angular.equals`.

It's during the `$digest` cycle that all watch expressions for a scope object are evaluated. When a watch expression detects that a `$scope` property has changed, then a listener function is fired.

Occasionally a property is changed without AngularJS knowing about it, and at that time you can manually kick off a digest cycle via `$apply`. The most common reason for this is that you've made an API call or a third-party library has done something that AngularJS needs to know about (see figure 3.7).

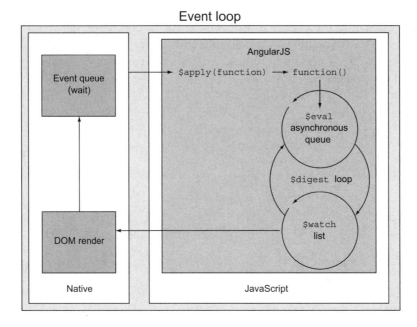

Figure 3.7   The academic digest cycle

3.3.2 Controller as syntax

In AngularJS 1.3, a new convention was introduced for working with controllers known as the *controller-as* syntax. In a hypothetical situation, instead of declaring a controller on the view as `ng-controller="StoryboardCtrl"`, you'd define it as `ng-controller="StoryboardCtrl as storyboard"`. Throughout the rest of the view, you'd refer to that controller as *storyboard*. For instance, if you wanted to bind to `someProperty` that existed on the controller, it would look like `{{storyboard.someProperty}}` and not `{{someProperty}}`.

This new syntax accomplishes two things: it reduces ambiguity in the markup about where a property is coming from and hedges the bad habit of implicitly inheriting from scope. All scope objects prototypically inherit from their parent scope object all the way up to `$rootScope`. If a property or method was referenced on a controller and it didn't exist, AngularJS would go up the scope's prototype chain until it found what it was looking for. A lazy developer would be okay relying on the existence of a property or method on a parent scope, because it would appear to be convenient at first. This unfortunately is a recipe for disaster and all kinds of unpredictable behavior when various entities start to manipulate shared data with no understanding of how it's being used elsewhere in the application.

In the simplest terms, the controller-as syntax creates a variable on scope and binds it to the actual instance of the controller function. This allows you to attach methods and properties directly to the instance in the form of `this.someProperty` or `this.someMethod`.

Continuing with our hypothetical scenario, you can see in the following code how this would work:

> **We store a top-level reference to this, which is a common JavaScript pattern and useful if you run into scoping issues—purely optional, but also convenient.**

> **When you use controller-as syntax, you don't need to inject $scope unless you need it for a specific purpose like eventing.**

> **Here we define a property and method directly on the instance of the controller.**

> **We can also define properties directly on $scope.**

> **We'll log this out to the console to see what's happening under the hood.**

```
angular.module('Angello.Storyboard')
    .controller('StoryboardCtrl', function($scope) {
        var storyboard = this;

        storyboard.someProperty = 'My property';
        storyboard.someMethod = function() {
            // Do something;
        };

        $scope.scopeProperty = 'Scope property';

        console.log('$scope', $scope);
    });
```

As you can see from the console log in figure 3.8, AngularJS just created a variable on scope for the name we used when we defined our controller using controller-as syntax. All of our properties and methods then get defined on the storyboard object,

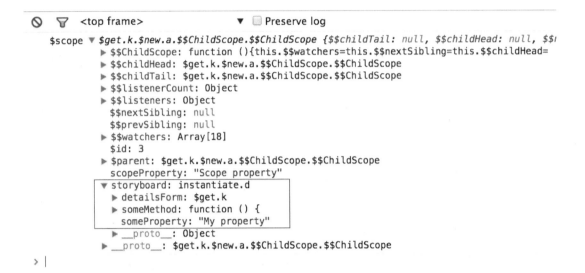

Figure 3.8 Console output of controller-as

which is bound to $scope under the hood. Therefore, the controller for each view in an application is instantiated as an object that is itself a property of $scope. Note that the scopeProperty we defined on $scope is on the same level of storyboard.

This syntax is entirely optional, but the AngularJS team encourages people to use it because it allows you to write more precise views, and it significantly simplifies your controllers by eliminating the need for $scope.

3.3.3   *AngularJS events*

AngularJS has an event system that's useful for raising particular events and then responding to them elsewhere in the application (see table 3.1). The two ways of sending an event are $broadcast and $emit, which differ only in the direction the event is going. Listening and responding to a specific event is handled by $on.

Table 3.1 Events in AngularJS

Event	Behavior
$broadcast	Sends events from a parent scope *downward* to its children.
$emit	Sends events from a child *upward* to its parent.
$on	Listens for an event and responds.

Using events requires the presence of a scope object, which means that if you want to broadcast an event from a service, you need to inject $rootScope. It's generally best practice to avoid using $rootScope directly, but the one place where it comes in really handy is when it's operating as an event bus. $broadcast sends an event from parent to child, so you're guaranteed that all scope objects will have an opportunity to respond to the event because all scope objects are under $rootScope in hierarchy.

Because of the presence of a scope object, most developers prefer to use promises to handle asynchronous events in their services.

3.4 *Properties and expressions*

At the core of this chapter, we're really trying to demonstrate how to do two things: bind to properties and execute expressions. We'll show the various ways to do that as we build out the storyboard view in Angello.

> **IT'S SIMPLER THAN IT MAY SEEM** AngularJS can seem fairly overwhelming when you first start using it, but as time goes on, you'll tend to see it in these simple terms. Most of what a developer does in AngularJS comes down to binding to properties and executing expressions.

3.4.1 *Display stories with ngRepeat*

How would you take a collection of objects and display them on the page without having to define a layout for each item? Wouldn't it be nice if you could define a template once and then just repeat it over and over for each item in the collection? This is exactly the role that ngRepeat was designed to play.

We'll set the stage by defining the data structures that we're going to be working with for this example. We have a stories array that contains story objects as well as a statuses array that we'll use to define our status columns in the view:

```
// client/src/angello/storyboard/controllers/StoryboardController.js
angular.module('Angello.Storyboard')
    .controller('StoryboardCtrl', function() {
        var storyboard = this;

        storyboard.stories = [
            {
                "assignee": "1",
                "criteria": "It tests!",
                "description": "This is a test",
                "id": "1",
                "reporter": "2",
                "status": "To Do",
                "title": "First Story",
                "type": "Spike"
            },
            {
                "assignee": "2",
                "criteria": "It works!",
                "description": "testing something",
                "id": "2",
                "reporter": "1",
                "status": "In Progress",
                "title": "Second Story",
```

```
            "type": "Enhancement"
        }
    ];

    storyboard.statuses = [
        {name: 'To Do'},
        {name: 'In Progress'},
        {name: 'Code Review'},
        {name: 'QA Review'},
        {name: 'Verified'}
    ];
});
```

We'll start out by creating a column for each status in storyboard.statuses using ngRepeat on an ul element. The ngRepeat directive duplicates the element that it was declared on for each item in the collection that's providing data to the directive. Because it duplicates the child elements as well, we can define the layout once and just repeat it over and over. The expression "status in storyboard.statuses" essentially is telling AngularJS to repeat over the storyboard.statuses array, assign each item in the array, and refer to the current item in the iteration as status. This allows us to bind to a specific item in the array within the template, for example, {{status.name}}:

> **SCOPING** AngularJS is able to keep the instances of each item separate by implicitly creating a child scope for each template that's created by ngRepeat. Scope does an excellent job of providing context, so you don't have to worry about those types of things colliding.

```html
<!-- client/src/angello/storyboard/tmpl/storyboard.html -->
<div class="list-area">
    <div class="list-wrapper">
        <ul class="list"
            ng-repeat="status in storyboard.statuses">
            <h3 class="status">{{status.name}}</h3>
        <hr/>
        </ul>
    </div>
</div>
```

Because we have five statuses in the storyboard.statuses array, the final result is five columns with the status name on top (shown in figure 3.9).

Figure 3.9   The status columns

We'll nest another `ngRepeat` within our first `ngRepeat` to add a list item for every story in `storyboard.stories`:

```html
<!-- client/src/angello/storyboard/tmpl/storyboard.html -->
<div class="list-area">
    <div class="list-wrapper">
        <ul class="list"
            ng-repeat="status in storyboard.statuses">
            <h3 class="status">{{status.name}}</h3>
            <hr/>
            <li class="story"
                ng-repeat="story in storyboard.stories">
                <article>
                    <div>
                        <button type="button" class="close">x</button>
                        <p class="title">{{story.title}}</p>
                    </div>
                    <div class="type-bar {{story.type}}"></div>
                    <div>
                        <p>{{story.description}}</p>
                    </div>
                </article>
            </li>
        </ul>
    </div>
</div>
```

We'll use the same convention as before and define our second `ngRepeat` as `ng-repeat="story in storyboard.stories"`, which will loop over the `storyboard.stories` array and create a reference to each individual element as `story`. We then will use that reference to bind to and display `story.title` and `story.description`, as well as assign a class based on `story.type`.

One-way data binding

Two-way data binding is one of the major selling points of AngularJS, but there's a memory and overhead loss when using this feature. AngularJS 1.3 to the rescue! AngularJS 1.3 introduces a one-time binding feature that allows you to flag collections and values that only need to be evaluated once. Simply place two colons before the collection or value you want to bind once to.

```html
// client/src/angello/storyboard/tmpl/storyboard.html
<ul class="list my-repeat-animation"
    ng-repeat="status in ::storyboard.statuses">
    <h3 class="status">{{::status.name}}</h3>
    <!-- … -->
</ul>
```

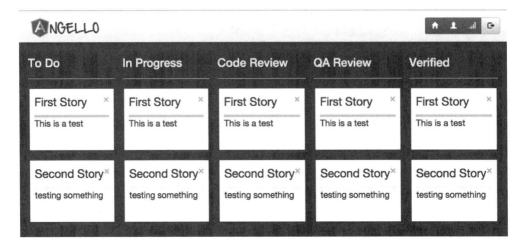

Figure 3.10   Stories in every column

The result (shown in figure 3.10) is that we've created a story element for each story in each of the status columns. This is obviously visually incorrect; we need a way to filter what we're displaying to show only the stories that match the status of the column they're in.

> ### Scope properties on ng-repeat
> There are some special properties created on the local scope of each `ng-repeat` instance. These include `$index`, `$first`, and `$even`, among others. Here's an example of how you could implement a simple expand/contract feature:
>
> ```
> // Hypothetical Scenario
> <ul>
>     <li ng-repeat="item in items"
>         ng-click="ctrl.currentIndex == $index" >
>         <h2>{{item.title}}</h2>
>         <p ng-if="ctrl.currentIndex == $index">
>             {{item.longDescription}}
>         </p>
>     </li>
> </ul>
> ```

3.4.2   *Filters*

Filters allow you to filter the contents of a collection to give you exactly what you want based on some sort of predefined criteria. In our case, we want to filter the `stories` array to return only the `stories` that match the `status` that we're currently on.

In AngularJS, you can modify the contents of an `ngRepeat` by adding a pipe symbol and then declaring a filter and what you want to use as your criteria. This looks like

Using ng-repeat to iterate over an object

In addition to using `ng-repeat` to iterate over a collection, you can use it to iterate over an object. This is effected by changing the syntax with which the `ng-repeat` is declared; for instance, suppose that stories were not a collection of objects but they were an object of objects. You could change up your declaration syntax a bit and gain access to the key as well as the value:

```
// Hypothetical Scenario
<ul>
    <li ng-repeat="(key, item) in items">
        <h2>{{key}}</h2>
        <h3>{{item.title}}</h3>
    </li>
</ul>
```

`| filter: {status:status.name}` in the following code. We're telling AngularJS to return only the stories where its `status` property matches the value of `status.name`:

```
<!-- client/src/angello/storyboard/tmpl/storyboard.html -->
<div class="list-area">
    <div class="list-wrapper">
        <ul class="list"
            ng-repeat="status in storyboard.statuses">
            <h3 class="status">{{status.name}}</h3>
            <hr/>
            <li class="story"
                ng-repeat="story in storyboard.stories
                    | filter: {status:status.name}">
                <article>
                    <div>
                        <button type="button" class="close">x</button>
                        <p class="title">{{story.title}}</p>
                    </div>
                    <div class="type-bar {{story.type}}"></div>
                    <div>
                        <p>{{story.description}}</p>
                    </div>
                </article>
            </li>
        </ul>
    </div>
</div>
```

This results in a much more useful rendering of the interface, as seen in figure 3.11.

We've managed to create a fairly sophisticated layout in approximately 20 lines of code using two instances of `ngRepeat` and a filter. Now you'll learn how to interact

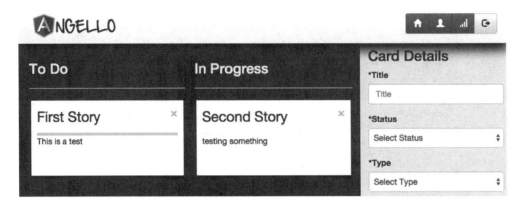

Figure 3.11   Stories filtered by status

with a story on an individual level as we start to add CRUD functionality to our storyboard view.

3.4.3   *Expressions*

As simple as it sounds, the foundation of great applications is the ability to capture and convey user interactions with the appropriate data and context. AngularJS comes with some powerful built-in directives to capture these user interactions, such as ngClick, ngBlur, ngFocus, ngSubmit, and so on. AngularJS also captures user interactions by binding the input of form elements to a data structure using ngModel. This allows for the implicit two-way data binding of an input to a property in your controller so that changes are automatically propagated.

In the following sections, you'll learn how to use the AngularJS interaction directives to call expressions that you expose on your controller to perform units of work. You'll use these elements to build out the standard *CRUD* (create, read, update, and delete) functionality for the storyboard.

DISPLAY A STORY'S DETAILS

You've learned how to display the stories collection with a template and ngRepeat and arrange them into columns using a filter, but how do you work with individual stories? If you're going to create or update a story, then you need the ability to display and modify the individual properties of each story object.

```
// client/src/angello/storyboard/controllers/StoryboardController.js
angular.module('Angello.Storyboard')
    .controller('StoryboardCtrl', function() {
        var storyboard = this;

        storyboard.currentStory = null;          ⟵  We store a reference to the
        storyboard.editedStory = {};             ⟵      currently selected story.
```

We store a reference to the currently selected story.

We also store a reference to a copy of the currently selected story so that we can edit it without affecting the original.

```
//...
```

This method gets called when a story is selected in the view.

```
storyboard.setCurrentStory = function(story) {
    storyboard.currentStory = story;
    storyboard.editedStory =
        angular.copy(storyboard.currentStory);
};
});
```

The story parameter gets assigned to the currentStory property.

We then use angular.copy to store a copy of currentStory as editedStory.

To capture when a user selects a story, we'll attach ngClick to the story template, which will call storyboard.setCurrentStory with the story object that was selected as a parameter:

```html
<!-- client/src/angello/storyboard/tmpl/storyboard.html -->
<li class="story"
    ng-repeat="story in storyboard.stories
        | filter: {status:status.name}"
    ng-click="storyboard.setCurrentStory(story)">
    <article>
        <div>
            <button type="button" class="close">x</button>
            <p class="title">{{story.title}}</p>
        </div>
        <div class="type-bar {{story.type}}"></div>
        <div>
            <p>{{story.description}}</p>
        </div>
    </article>
</li>
```

In the right side of the storyboard (shown in figure 3.12), we have a column with a form in it. When we select a story, we'll bind that form to the individual properties of the currently selected story.

The storyboard.detailsForm consists of mainly two types of inputs: text inputs and select controls. We'll examine one instance of each and in doing so will establish fairly well how the rest of the form is working.

The simplest element to work with in an AngularJS form is a text input, because you can bind the value of the input to a property using ngModel. To display and edit the title of the story we're editing, we can use the directive ng-model="storyboard.editedStory.title". When we enter a new value in that field, the value of storyboard.editedStory.title is instantly updated in the controller:

```html
<!-- client/src/angello/storyboard/tmpl/storyboard.html -->
<div class="details">
    <h3>Card Details</h3>
    <form name="storyboard.detailsForm">
        <div class="form-group">
            <div class="controls">
                <label class="control-label" for="inputTitle">*Title</label>
```

```
        <input type="text" id="inputTitle" name="inputTitle"
            placeholder="Title"
            ➡   ng-model="storyboard.editedStory.title"
            ng-required="true" ng-minlength="3" ng-maxlength="30"
            class="form-control">
      </div>
    </div>
    <!-- ... -->
  </form>
</div>
```

We can also do the same for a select control using `ngModel` in the form of `ng-model="storyboard.editedStory.reporter"`. A select control is significantly more complex than a simple text input, and so we don't have the luxury of just binding to a string value to populate it. We could technically populate a select control

Figure 3.12　Story details

using ngRepeat, but AngularJS provides a similar directive called ngOptions that was created specifically for populating options in a select control:

```
<!-- client/src/angello/storyboard/tmpl/storyboard.html -->
<select id="inputReporter" name="inputReporter"
        ng-model="storyboard.editedStory.reporter" ng-required="true"
        ng-options="user.id as user.name for user in storyboard.users"
        class="form-control">
    <option value="">Please select...</option>
</select>
```

The ngOptions directive works in a way similar to its ngRepeat cousin in that we start out with the same basic declaration that looks like user in storyboard.users. There are a few extra things that we want to define, such as what to use as the label and value. To define the label that's displayed, we need to extend that statement to look like user.name for user in storyboard.users, which means we'll use the user.name property as the label. Because we're storing the identity of storyboard.reporter as an id that exists in the storyboard.users array, we'll explicitly set the selected value to work with that property. This will create the final version of this statement to look like ng-options="user.id as user.name for user in storyboard.users". This allows us to immediately select that appropriate user in the dropdown based on a match between storyboard.editedStory.reporter and storyboard.users.id.

UPDATE A STORY

As we update elements in storyboard.detailsForm, the values are immediately reflected in storyboard.editedStory. With that in mind, to make our changes permanent, we just need to copy the updated properties back to the storyboard.current-Story reference. At the bottom of our form, we have a div that contains a button to update the story, and another to cancel the update altogether. We'll show this div when storyboard.currentStory is not null.

```
<!-- client/src/angello/storyboard/tmpl/storyboard.html -->
<div class="details">
    <h3>Card Details</h3>
    <form name="storyboard.detailsForm">
        <!-- ... -->
    </form>
    <hr/>
    <div ng-if="storyboard.currentStory">
        <button class="btn btn-default"
            ng-click="storyboard.updateCancel()">
            Cancel
        </button>
        <button class="btn pull-right btn-default"
                ng-disabled="!storyboard.detailsForm.$valid"
                ng-click="storyboard.updateStory()">Update Story</button>
    </div>
    <!-- ... -->
</div>
```

We'll use ngClick to call storyboard.updateCancel if we want to cancel, and story-board.updateStory to complete the update. Calling updateCancel calls resetForm, which we covered previously. The updateStory method is interesting in that we have an array of properties that we want to update and we're iterating over them and copying them back to the storyboard.currentStory object. Once we've done that, we call resetForm to clean up after ourselves:

```
// client/src/angello/storyboard/controllers/StoryboardController.js
angular.module('Angello.Storyboard')
    .controller('StoryboardCtrl', function() {
        //...

        storyboard.updateStory = function() {
            var fields = ['title', 'description', 'criteria',
                          'status', 'type', 'reporter', 'assignee'];

            fields.forEach(function(field) {
                storyboard.currentStory[field]
                    = storyboard.editedStory[field];
            });

            storyboard.resetForm();
        };

        storyboard.updateCancel = function() {
            storyboard.resetForm();
        };

        storyboard.resetForm = function() {
            storyboard.currentStory = null;
            storyboard.editedStory = {};

            storyboard.detailsForm.$setPristine();
            storyboard.detailsForm.$setUntouched();
        };
    });
```

The updateStory method gets called when a story is currently selected and the Update button is clicked.

We iterate over an array of property names and copy the property values corresponding to those names from the editedStory back to the currentStory.

If the user wants to cancel the update, we just need to call resetForm.

This method resets the currentStory and editedStory properties as well as resets the detailsForm back into a pristine, untouched state.

CREATE A STORY

Creating a story works almost exactly like updating a story except that we don't have a current story selected. When storyboard.currentStory is null, we hide the update controls and show the button to create a new story:

```
<!-- client/src/angello/storyboard/tmpl/storyboard.html -->
<div class="details">
    <h3>Card Details</h3>
    <form name="storyboard.detailsForm">
        <!-- ... -->
    </form>
    <hr/>
    <!-- ... -->
    <div ng-if="!storyboard.currentStory">
        <button class="btn pull-right btn-default"
                ng-disabled="!storyboard.detailsForm.$valid"
                ng-click="storyboard.createStory()">
```

```
            Create Story
        </button>
    </div>
</div>
```

The `createStory` method creates a copy of the `storyboard.editedStory` and pushes it into the `storyboard.stories` array as a new story. And just like `updateStory`, we're calling `resetForm` to reset everything:

```
// client/src/angello/storyboard/controllers/StoryboardController.js
angular.module('Angello.Storyboard')
    .controller('StoryboardCtrl', function() {
        //...

        // Utility function for this example
        function ID() {
            return '_' + Math.random().toString(36).substr(2, 9);
        };

        storyboard.createStory = function() {
            var newStory = angular.copy(storyboard.editedStory);
            newStory.id = ID();

            storyboard.stories.push(newStory);
            storyboard.resetForm();
        };
        //...
    });
```

> This is a utility method to generate a unique ID. In real life, this would get generated by the database.

> This method creates a copy of editedStory which, because of AngularJS data binding, contains as properties all the new form values that have just been selected or typed into the form, and then assigns a generated ID to the new story. We then push it into the stories array and call resetForm to reset the form.

SUGAR Because array management isn't straightforward in JavaScript, we're using a utility library to manipulate collections until we hook up the application to a server-side technology that will handle that for us. We used Sugar.js in Angello because it makes working with arrays feel like how we wish they worked in the first place. With that said, you can accomplish the same thing with Lodash or Underscore.

DELETE A STORY

We'll round out the CRUD circuit by adding the ability to delete a `story` from the `storyboard.stories` collection. We create a method called `deleteStory` that accepts a story ID, and we'll use a Sugar.js method to actually remove the `story` object from the `stories` array:

```
angular.module('Angello.Storyboard')
    .controller('StoryboardCtrl', function() {
        //...

        storyboard.deleteStory = function(storyId) {
            storyboard.stories.remove(function(story) {
```

> The deleteStory method is called with the ID of the story we want to delete.

> We use the Sugar.js remove method to remove the story from the stories array based on the value of storyId.

```
                    return story.id === storyId;
                });

                storyboard.resetForm();
            };
        });
```

As a matter of housecleaning, we're calling `resetForm` after the story has been deleted. Now that we've created and exposed the method for deleting a story, we can call `delete-Story` with `ngClick` and pass in the `story.id` for the story we want to delete:

```html
<!-- client/src/angello/storyboard/tmpl/storyboard.html -->
<!-- although illustrating a slightly different implementation -->
<li class="story"
    ng-repeat="story in storyboard.stories
        | filter: {status:status.name}"
    ng-click="storyboard.setCurrentStory(story)">
    <article>
        <div>
            <button type="button" class="close"
                    ng-click="storyboard.deleteStory(story.id)">
        ➥      x</button>
            <p class="title">{{story.title}}</p>
        </div>
        <div class="type-bar {{story.type}}"></div>
        <div>
            <p>{{story.description}}</p>
        </div>
    </article>
</li>
```

3.5   *Best practices and testing*

Now that you've seen several examples of what you can do with views and controllers, let's take a moment to cover some best practices as well as how to test a controller.

Controllers should be lightweight and specific to the view they control. Controllers are responsible for receiving data from services and processing it for display in the view, as well as communicating data back to services for logic processing. It's generally a bad sign when you have a "fat" controller that's performing large amounts of logic to transform data based on a user's input. Those units of logic should first be examined for opportunities to simplify and then be promoted to a service, so that the controller is acting more as a communicator or a mediator between the view and the services the view interacts with.

Controllers should have no knowledge of the view they control. If this is executed correctly, it's entirely possible to use one controller for many views. This works well if a view is a subset of another view. Isolating the controller from the view makes testing the controller significantly easier, since you're not dependent on a browser to render operational DOM elements in conjunction with trying to execute JavaScript.

A lot of developers new to testing find the most challenging part is figuring out how to initialize the particular piece of code they want to test. Let's step through how we initialize `StoryboardCtrl` to see how this can be approached:

We create a placeholder for the controller we're going to initialize.

Using the module object from ngMock, we initialize the Angello.Storyboard module.

Inject the $controller service so that we can initialize our controller.

Because StoryboardCtrl has no dependencies, we initialize it with an empty object and store a reference to it on the ctrl variable.

Forms implicitly create properties and methods on controllers, so we mock out just enough of the ctrl.detailsForm object for our tests to pass.

```
// client/tests/specs/controllers/StoryboardController.spec.js
describe('StoryboardCtrl', function() {
    var ctrl;

    beforeEach(module('Angello.Storyboard'));

    beforeEach(inject(function($controller) {
        ctrl = $controller('StoryboardCtrl', {});
        ctrl.detailsForm = {
            $setPristine: function() { },
            $setUntouched: function() {   }
        };
    }));
});
```

With the `StoryboardCtrl` properly initialized and stored as a reference, testing it becomes a lot like pressing buttons on a calculator and making sure that everything adds up. For instance, when we call `ctrl.resetForm`, the result is that `ctrl.current-Story` is null and `ctrl.editedStory` is an empty object. This is the expected end result, and in order to make sure that `ctrl.resetForm` is working, we'll set `ctrl.editedStory` and `ctrl.currentStory` to an arbitrary value, which in this case is `{assignee: '1'}`. We can then call `ctrl.resetForm`, and then assert our expected outcome through our Jasmine[1] assertions:

```
// client/tests/specs/controllers/StoryboardController.spec.js
it('should reset the form', function() {
    ctrl.editedStory = ctrl.currentStory = {assignee: '1'};

    ctrl.resetForm();

    expect(ctrl.currentStory).toBeNull();
    expect(ctrl.editedStory).toEqual({});
});
```

Let's examine one more test for good measure. When we delete a `story`, the expected outcome is that the `story` is no longer in the `ctrl.stories` collection. We set the stage by storing a reference to the first `story` in the `ctrl.stories` array. Using that

---

[1] Jasmine is a behavior-driven development framework for testing JavaScript code; see http://jasmine .github.io/2.0/introduction.html.

story reference, we then call `ctrl.deleteStory` and pass in the ID of the `story` reference we just made. In Jasmine, we can make an assertion negative by adding `not` as a prefix to the assertion. Because we want to make sure that `ctlr.stories` doesn't contain the story we just deleted, we can use the assertion `.not.toContain(story)` to test for that condition:

```
// client/tests/specs/controllers/StoryboardController.spec.js
it('should delete a story', function() {
    var story = ctrl.stories[0];

    ctrl.deleteStory(story.id);

    expect(ctrl.stories).not.toContain(story);
});
```

3.6   *Summary*

Understanding how views and controllers work—and more importantly how they relate to each other—is the foundation for understanding AngularJS. Much of the prototype work that we do starts with a simple view and controller, and as we achieve the desired functionality, we'll start to refactor out the view to directives and the controller to services.

Let's review what we've covered so far before we move on to the next chapter:

- A view is the HTML after it has been through the AngularJS compilation process.
- A controller is responsible for defining methods and properties on scope so that they're available to the view.
- Scope in AngularJS is simply a JavaScript object that has some events built into it so that the view and controller can be synchronized. It's essentially the glue between the view and controller.
- The new controller-as syntax simplifies our controllers by implicitly assigning the controller instance to the scope itself.
- When a property is declared on scope, it's immediately available for binding in the view.
- When a method is declared on scope, it's available to be called from the view.
- AngularJS comes with prebuilt directives that you can use to perform operations such as `ngRepeat` for iterating over a collection and displaying each instance with a template or `ngClick` for capturing a mouse click and calling a method on the controller.
- You can use filters to filter out items in a collection in `ngRepeat` so that you only display a subset of the original array, as you saw in the case of our storyboard columns.

Models and services 4

This chapter covers

- The vital role that models and services play
- Different types of services and how to create them
- Using $http to communicate with remote servers
- How promises handle asynchronous communication
- Using $http interceptors
- How to use decorators to enhance services
- Testing models and services

If a controller is supposed to be lightweight and only concern itself with the view it's controlling, what happens when you need functionality to be available to your entire application? If a controller should never communicate directly with other controllers, how do they share information? Whereas controllers are constrained to a specific context, AngularJS services exist to provide functionality that's available to the entire application.

In this chapter we'll explore what a service is and how to create a simple service. From there, we'll show how to use services to communicate with a remote server and serve as a domain model for the entire application. After that we'll dip our toes

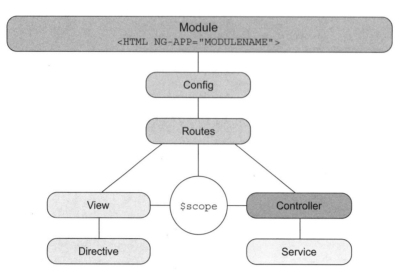

Figure 4.1 Services and the big picture

into some advanced functionality and see how to intercept remote server calls as well as decorate existing services. Figure 4.1 shows a high-level view of services.

4.1 *What are models and services?*

Before we start digging into the technical underpinnings of how services work in AngularJS and all of the amazing things you can do with them, we need to agree on some semantics. The phrase *service* is admittedly an overloaded term in AngularJS that can lead to some confusion, especially if you're coming from other languages. Technically, a service in AngularJS is any piece of common functionality that can be shared across your entire application. In quite a few other languages, a "service" refers to a mechanism that communicates with a remote service, whereas a "model" is responsible for not only communicating with the remote service but managing the state surrounding that data.

For the course of this book, we'll refer to a *service* in the most generic AngularJS sense, in that a service may or may not communicate with a remote service, but it's available to provide some functionality to the application. It's a service to the application, and one or more of these services may contain the model on which the application relies for its data. We'll refer to any service that communicates with a remote service and manages that state as a *model*.

> **TEAM TALK** Don't get hung up too much on this, as it's just semantics, but it's extremely helpful to agree on what exactly a service means when you're communicating with your team.

4.1.1 Hello services

Services are ultimately registered with the application with the built-in $provide service, but in most cases it's easier to use the syntactic sugar provided by angular.module. These convenience methods are module.value, module.constant, module.service, module.factory, and module.provider. We'll get into each of these methods in this chapter, but let's start out by creating a simple service to define the available story types and then make it available in the StoryboardCtrl.

In the Angello.js file, we'll register a value that will be available as a service throughout the application via myModule.value, give it a name of STORY_TYPES, and pass in an array of objects as the second parameter:

```
// client/src/angello/Angello.js
myModule.value('STORY_TYPES', [
    {name: 'Feature'},
    {name: 'Enhancement'},
    {name: 'Bug'},
    {name: 'Spike'}
]);
```

And now the STORY_TYPES service is available for injection anywhere in the Angello application:

```
// client/src/angello/storyboard/controllers/StoryboardController.js
angular.module('Angello.Storyboard')
    .controller('StoryboardCtrl',
        function (STORY_TYPES) {
        var myStory = this;

        //...

        myStory.types = STORY_TYPES;

        //...
    });
```

In the StoryboardController.js file, we're injecting STORY_TYPES into StoryboardCtrl. We then make the story types service available to the view by attaching it to the controller via myStory.types = STORY_TYPES. The beauty of extracting the different story types into a service is that we can pass it into any other controller, directive, and even another service without having to redefine it. For instance, we use STORY_TYPES in our dashboard view when we're generating our graphs. Define once, use everywhere.

4.1.2 The service lifecycle

Now that you've seen a service in action, let's take a moment to talk about the actual lifecycle of a service.

The lifecycle is as follows:

1 A service is defined on angular.module using one of the convenience functions, or in some cases directly with $provide.

2   During the compilation cycle, services are then registered in an instance factory for creation.

3   When a service is required, the $injector service will check the instance cache to see if an instance of the requested service exists. If it does, $injector will use the instance from cache and inject it into whatever requested the service. If not, $injector will request a new instance from the instance factory and then return the new instance after it has stored it in cache for future retrieval. See figure 4.2.

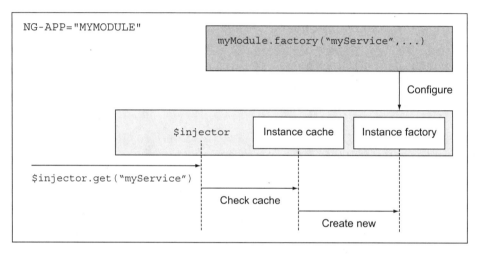

Figure 4.2 Service lifecycle

There are two important things to note about the lifecycle of a service: a service doesn't get loaded until something requests it, and a service only gets instantiated once, making it an application singleton. The service object is passed by reference into every controller that needs access to it. There are a few ways around this, but the necessity to create multiple instances of a service is an edge case at best. Keeping a single source of truth is a good thing!

4.1.3   The different types of services

There are five different ways to define a service, as shown in table 4.1. In the following sections, we'll cover the differences between the five and which one is appropriate for different situations.

Table 4.1   When to use which service module

Type	Reason
module.value	Good for storing simple values that may need to change during runtime.
module.constant	Good for storing simple values that will never need to change.

Table 4.1 When to use which service module *(continued)*

Type	Reason
module.service	Creates a service using a constructor method. This is good for developers who prefer OOP-style programming and like using the this keyword.
module.factory	Creates a service using a constructor function. Developers using the Revealing Module pattern will be at home with this style.
module.provider	Provides the most control over defining your service but is more complex and verbose. Good for modifying behavior of a service while the application is being configured.

VALUE SERVICE

The simplest of all services is a *value service*. The value service method takes two parameters: the name of the service and the value that is to be returned when the value service is instantiated. This can be a primitive value, object, or even a function.

```
// client/src/angello/Angello.js
myModule.value('STORY_TYPES', [
    {name: 'Feature'},
    {name: 'Enhancement'},
    {name: 'Bug'},
    {name: 'Spike'}
]);
```

And we consume STORY_TYPES by injecting it into our StoryboardController:

```
// client/src/angello/storyboard/controllers/StoryboardController.js
angular.module('Angello.Storyboard')
    .controller('StoryboardCtrl',
        function (STORY_TYPES) {
        var myStory = this;

        //...

        myStory.types = STORY_TYPES;

        //...
    });
```

Value services are limited in the sense that they can't be accessed in the module.config block during compilation. With that said, they can be modified during the application lifecycle.

CONSTANT SERVICE

A *constant service* is similar to a value service except that it's available to the module .config block and can't be modified during runtime. Constant services are especially handy for configuration values that aren't going to change during the course of the application lifecycle.

For instance, we can use the constant service to define a remote URI like the following:

```
// client/src/angello/app/services/EndpointConfigService.js
angular.module('Angello.Common')
    .constant('CURRENT_BACKEND', 'firebase');
```

This allows us to encapsulate our back-end choice into a single place and pass it around as needed.

SERVICE CONSTRUCTOR AND SERVICE FACTORY

The most common type of a service is one created by a service constructor or a service factory. We'll examine these together because the distinction between the two is subtle and really comes down to stylistic preference.

> **SERVICE FAULT** This is another case where the term *service* creates awkwardness because it's overloaded. A service-defined service, anyone?

When you define a service using `module.service`, the instance is returned via a constructor function. This lends itself well to developers who prefer writing object-oriented code and like to define methods and properties on the `this` keyword.

```
// client/src/angello/app/services/LoadingService.js
angular.module('Angello.Common')
    .service('LoadingService',
        function ($rootScope) {
            var service = this;

            service.setLoading = function (loading) {
                $rootScope.loadingView = loading;
            };
        });
```

In the preceding code, we've defined the `LoadingService` that's responsible for setting the `loadingView` variable on `$rootScope` that controls the loading modal in Angello. Note that we've created a variable called `service` and assigned it the value of `this`. The reason we've done this is because `this` is a context-sensitive value, and it's a common technique to store the top-level function reference to `this` so that it can be accessed within children function blocks.

Now we'll show the same service using `module.factory` to declare the Loading-Service. This works in exactly the same way as the previous service, but it returns an object that exposes methods and properties:

```
angular.module('Angello.Common')
    .factory('LoadingService',
        function ($rootScope) {
            var setLoading = function (loading) {
                $rootScope.loadingView = loading;
            };

            return {
                setLoading: setLoading
            }
        });
```

This is very similar to the Revealing Module design pattern, in that only the methods and properties that you expose on the return object are publicly accessible. This is a great way to delineate between public and private members of a service.

The differences between these two services are nearly indistinguishable to anything that consumes them, so you're able to use the style that you're most comfortable with.

PROVIDER FUNCTION

The provider function is the core method for defining a service, and the most verbose. In most cases it's unnecessary to define a service using `module.provider` unless you need to add additional configuration during the configuration phase of your application. An example of this is if you need to share a service across multiple applications but also want to introduce application-specific behavior during compilation. Though we haven't used `module.provider` directly in Angello, we'll configure built-in providers when we get into `$http` *interceptors* and *service decorators*.

> **FURTHER READING** We've done our best to keep everything anchored to specific code in the application, but if you want to read more about the different types of services, check out the docs at the following links:
>
> https://docs.angularjs.org/api/auto/service/$provide
>
> https://docs.angularjs.org/guide/providers

4.2 *Models with $http*

Applications don't live in a vacuum—especially not web applications—so we'll transition from services to models. We need a way to persist data outside of the client, and that involves communicating with a remote server. AngularJS makes server-side communication easy with the built-in `$http` service, and in this section we'll walk through a fully functional model built around `$http`.

> **BACK END** We've tried to shield the actual server-side code from this chapter as much as possible so we could focus on AngularJS. For the absolute minimal amount of setup to get Angello running, we recommend using Firebase, but have also provided a Node.js back end that you can run locally. You can find instructions on how to get up and running with either solution in the appendixes. The goal is that you simply need to change the CURRENT_BACKEND constant and provide your URI, and because both solutions provide a REST API, the application will work without having to change anything else.

4.2.1 *What is $http?*

`$http` is an AngularJS service that uses the browser's `XMLHttpRequest` object or JSONP to communicate with a remote server via HTTP. Server-side communication is asynchronous by nature, and `$http` is built with a deferred/promise API based on the `$q` service. We'll get into promises later in this chapter, but it's important to know that there's an elegant mechanism in place to handle sequencing asynchronous activities.

RESTful APIs provide a convention for communicating with remote servers that make the underlying technology of the remote server secondary. AngularJS embraces this and exposes convenience functions based on RESTful verbs and even goes a step further by creating a higher-level abstraction around REST with the $resource service.

> **LIMITED RESOURCE** We're not going to get into the $resource service in this book, but it's easy to pick up if you understand the concepts around $http.

4.2.2 *Create your first model*

We'll create our first model, StoriesModel, which calls the remote server and gets all of the stories for the logged-in user.

The first thing we'll do is define StoriesModel on the Angello.Common module using the service method. We'll pass in three dependencies—$http, AuthModel, and ENDPOINT_URI—to help set up communication to the remote server. The $http service will do the actual heavy lifting, with AuthModel and ENDPOINT_URI helping construct the appropriate URI for the call.

```
// client/src/angello/app/models/StoriesModel.js
angular.module('Angello.Common')
    .service('StoriesModel',
        function ($http, EndpointConfigService, UtilsService) {
            //...
        });
```

Now that we have all the ingredients to build out a proper model, we need to get a few things in order before we make the actual call:

```
// client/src/angello/app/models/StoriesModel.js
angular.module('Angello.Common')
    .service('StoriesModel',
        function ($http, EndpointConfigService, UtilsService) {
            var service = this,
                MODEL = "/stories/";

            //...
        });
```

The first thing we'll do is create a variable called service that's assigned the value of this. Then we'll create a variable called MODEL and assign a string that helps us create a proper URL.

And now it's time to construct the actual call to the server:

```
// client/src/angello/app/models/StoriesModel.js
angular.module('Angello.Common')
    .service('StoriesModel',
        function ($http, EndpointConfigService, UtilsService) {
            var service = this,
                MODEL = "/stories/";

            service.all = function () {
```

```
            return $http.get(EndpointConfigService.getUrl(
                MODEL + EndpointConfigService.getCurrentFormat()))
                    .then(
                        function(result) {
                            return UtilsService.objectToArray(result);
                        }
                    );
        };

        //...
    });
```

We'll do a GET request to the remote server to get all of the stories for the logged-in user's account. Because $http is built with REST convenience methods, the call will look like $http.get(YOUR_URL). The URL is created by the EndpointConfigService and is based on our MODEL variable and the CURRENT_BACKEND constant. We create and expose a method on the StoriesModel appropriately named all, which returns the results of calling $http.get.

We'll elaborate on how to handle the server response in greater depth when we get into promises, but we can see the general idea by examining the service call from the StoryboardCtrl:

```
// client/src/angello/storyboard/controllers/StoryboardController.js
storyboard.getStories = function () {
    StoriesModel.all()
        .then(function (result) {
            console.log(result.data);
        });
};
```

When getStories is executed, StoriesModel.all gets called and the result of that call is handled in the then method. The first parameter of the then method is the handler for a successful call and the first parameter of that handler is the result of that call. We can then see the actual data by calling console.log(result.data).

> **PROMISES** Promises can be a really tricky concept to wrap your mind around, and so they get an entire section in this chapter for explanation. For now, all you need to know is that when you call a method that returns an $http result, you can process the result with this bit of code:
>
> .then(function(result) { /* Handle result here */ });

4.2.3 *$http convenience methods*

You've seen a quick example of how to do GET requests to return a collection of user stories, but how do you do other useful things at the server level? How do you get a single user story? How do you create a user story? Update a user story? Delete one?

This is where the RESTful convenience methods provided by $http prove to be really helpful. You can actually call $http directly with a single configuration argument such as `$http({method: 'GET', url: '/someUrl'})`, but using the shortcut methods are easier to read and more self-documenting.

Using the acronym CRUD as a foundation, let's examine table 4.2, which shows the `$http` methods you'd call to engage this functionality.

Table 4.2   CRUD operations and `$http` methods

Operation	Method
Get all stories	`$http.get(EndpointConfigService.getUrl(MODEL + EndpointConfigService.getCurrentFormat()));`
Get a single story based on the `story_id`	`$http.get(EndpointConfigService.getUrlForId(MODEL, story_id));`
Create a story	`$http.post(EndpointConfigService.getUrl(MODEL + EndpointConfigService.getCurrentFormat()), story);`
Update a story based on the `story_id`	`$http.put(EndpointConfigService.getUrlForId(MODEL, story_id), story);`
Delete a story based on the `story_id`	`$http.delete(EndpointConfigService.getUrlForId(MODEL, story_id));`

Note that you call a function `getUrlForId` when dealing with calls that require interaction with a specific story. Because the URLs for dealing with the individuals calls are pretty much the same, creating `getUrl` and `getUrlForId` to generate the URLs for the actual calls reduces cruft in the service. If you need to change the URL structure, you can change the `CURRENT_BACKEND` constant in `EndpointConfigService.js` and the `MODEL` variable in the specific model file, and the change in URL structure is reflected in that entire service:

```
// client/src/angello/app/services/EndpointConfigService.js
angular.module('Angello.Common')
    //.constant('CURRENT_BACKEND', 'node')
    .constant('CURRENT_BACKEND', 'firebase')


// client/src/angello/app/models/StoriesModel.js
angular.module('Angello.Common')
    .service('StoriesModel',
        function ($http, EndpointConfigService, UtilsService) {
            var service = this,
                MODEL = "/stories/";

                //...
        });
```

And now `StoriesModel` in its entirety:

```
// client/src/angello/app/models/StoriesModel.js
angular.module('Angello.Common')
    .service('StoriesModel',
```

```
function ($http, EndpointConfigService, UtilsService) {
    var service = this,
        MODEL = "/stories/";

    service.all = function () {
        return $http.get(EndpointConfigService.getUrl(
            MODEL + EndpointConfigService.getCurrentFormat()))
                .then(
                    function(result) {
                        return UtilsService.objectToArray(result);
                    }
                );
    };

    service.fetch = function (story_id) {
        return $http.get(
            EndpointConfigService.getUrlForId(MODEL, story_id)
        );
    };

    service.create = function (story) {
        return $http.post(EndpointConfigService.getUrl(
            MODEL
                + EndpointConfigService.getCurrentFormat()), story
        );
    };

    service.update = function (story_id, story) {
        return $http.put(
            EndpointConfigService.getUrlForId(MODEL, story_id),
                story
        );
    };

    service.destroy = function (story_id) {
        return $http.delete(
            EndpointConfigService.getUrlForId(MODEL, story_id)
        );
    };
});
```

And in exactly 40 lines of code, we're able to realize complete CRUD functionality using two clever helper methods from EndpointConfigService.js to generate the appropriate URLs and the $http shortcut methods. Now that we've completed another lap around the track on how to call a remote service, let's get into how to handle the results with promises.

4.3   *Promises*

Calling a remote server is an asynchronous operation with no guarantee of when a response will be returned. How do you sequence code when you don't know precisely when things are going to happen? It would be nice if you could make your call and move on with your life until the call returned, and even better if the call would let you know when it was back. *Promises* are just the tool for the job!

4.3.1   What are promises?

Here's an illustration that makes promises a bit easier to visualize. Imagine you're in a restaurant where you walk up to the host and make a request for a table for you and all your friends. The host takes your name and gives you a buzzer to hold. When a table is ready, the buzzer will go off and you'll know that you're ready to be seated. You're not sitting near the door wringing your hands wondering if you're going to get seated, because you have the buzzer and it's definitely going to go off sometime in the future with the promise of a table.

And here we are! A promise is much like that buzzer at the restaurant. When you make a remote server call, a promise object is returned and patiently sits there until it's resolved and then performs whatever logic you desire. It's an object with a promise that it will be dealt with sometime in the future.

4.3.2   Promises in action

Let's anchor this freshly painted visual into actual code. We'll revisit the `$http.get` example we used previously and elaborate and then extend it.

Firstly, we need to set up our GET call to get all of the stories available for the logged-in user:

```
// client/src/angello/app/models/StoriesModel.js
service.all = function () {
    return $http.get(EndpointConfigService.getUrl(
            MODEL + EndpointConfigService.getCurrentFormat()))
                .then(
                    function(result) {
                        return UtilsService.objectToArray(result);
                    }
                );
};
```

The `service.all` method returns the result of `$http.get`, which is a promise object:

```
// client/src/angello/storyboard/controllers/StoryboardController.js
storyboard.getStories = function () {
    StoriesModel.all()
        .then(function (result) {
            storyboard.stories = (result !== 'null') ? result : {};
            $log.debug('RESULT', result);
        }, function (reason) {
            $log.debug('REASON', reason);
        });
};
```

The result of `StoriesModel.all` is essentially a promise object that has a `then` method that will get called when the `$http` call is resolved. The `then` method takes three function parameters that will get called at appropriate states of the promise. The three methods are the success callback, error callback, and notify callback. The success callback gets called when the promise is successfully resolved, whereas the error callback is called when the promise is rejected. The notify callback is called with an update to the value of the call.

Let's use the preceding code and break it down into pieces.

We call `StoriesModel.all` and then resolve it with the `then` method:

```
StoriesModel.all()
    .then();
```

From here we want to add in the success and error callbacks. The success callback takes a single parameter, which is the value of the server call. The error callback also gets a single parameter, which is a result object with information on the failed call:

```
StoriesModel.all()
    .then(function (result) {
    }, function (reason) {
    });
```

And now we can do something specific with regard to the `StoryBoardCtrl`. We'll assign `result.data` to `storyboard.stories` as well as log the result via `$log.debug`:

```
StoriesModel.all().then(function (result) {
        storyboard.stories = (result !== 'null') ? result : {};
        $log.debug('RESULT', result);
    }, function (reason) {
        $log.debug('REASON', reason);
    });
```

And in case something goes totally awry, we'll log the reason for the rejection with `$log.debug` as well.

The beauty of arriving at this point with a grasp on how we've constructed how we're handling the response is that we simply apply the pattern to other calls. For example, let's look at how we handle the response to `StoriesModel.update`:

```
StoriesModel.update(storyboard.currentStoryId, storyboard.editedStory)
    .then(function (result) {
        storyboard.getStories();
        storyboard.resetForm();
        $log.debug('RESULT', result);
    }, function (reason) {
        $log.debug('REASON', reason);
    });
```

It's exactly the same pattern!

4.3.3 *$http.success and $http.error*

Calling `$http` returns a promise object that has a `then` method, which we've covered up to this point, but there are two extra HTTP-specific methods called `success` and `error`.

Using .then(), .catch(), and .finally()

Angular 1.3 introduced a concept of using a `.then().catch().finally()` syntax to resolve promises instead of using just `.then()`. The choice is yours, as both methods work fine, but we find that the new syntax works better to articulate exactly what's going on. Here's a code snippet:

```
// Hypothetical Scenario
myPromise()
    .then(function(result) {
        // Success Callback
    })
    .catch(function(error) {
        // Error Callback
    })
    .finally(function() {
        // Gets executed no matter what
    })
;
```

The `success` and `error` methods work almost exactly like `then`, but the callbacks have additional parameters to give you more information about the HTTP call:

```
$http.get(EndpointConfigService.getUrl(
        MODEL + EndpointConfigService.getCurrentFormat())
    )
    .success(function(data, status, headers, config) {
      // this callback will be called asynchronously
      // when the response is available
    })
    .error(function(data, status, headers, config) {
      // called asynchronously if an error occurs
      // or server returns response with an error status.
    });
```

This is a convenient alternative if you need to perform extra logic specific to the HTTP call.

4.3.4   *Elegant sequencing with promises*

In the previous section, you learned that the return value of calling a method on `$http` is a promise object which has a `then` method to handle the response. What if you could create your own promise object and control when it was resolved or rejected? This would be useful if you needed to perform some transformative process on the result before making it available to the rest of the application. Another useful scenario is if you wanted to implement a caching mechanism to eliminate unnecessary calls to the server.

You'll learn a technique for caching the response and then manually resolving the promise if you already have it stored in the model. The annotations walk through the code in a way that mirrors the sequence of execution when it's run:

Our promise begins with a deferred object created by calling $q.defer. Though it's not visible in the code snippet, make sure to inject the $q service into your model.

We then return the promise object via return deferred.promise.

When we make a successful call to the server, we store the result for future use.

If something goes wrong with the call, we can pass in the deferred.reject method to handle that scenario.

```
service.all = function () {
    var deferred = $q.defer(); // $q will be explained shortly

    if(service.stories) {
        deferred.resolve(service.stories);
    } else {
        $http.get(EndpointConfigService.getUrl(
            MODEL + EndpointConfigService.getCurrentFormat())
        )
        .success(function(data, status, headers, config) {
            service.stories = data;
            deferred.resolve(service.stories);
        })
        .error(deferred.reject);
    }

    return deferred.promise;
};
```

We then tell the deferred object to resolve the promise with the service.stories value by calling deferred.resolve(service.stories).

This is where the caching mechanism comes into play. When service.all is called, we check to see if service.stories exists and, if so, we resolve the promise with the existing value. If not, then we go ahead and make that initial server call.

By using a deferred object directly, you can resolve a promise whenever you see fit. You now have the ability to insert a level of logic between the server call and the moment when the rest of the application has an opportunity to respond to the result of that call.

4.4 *$http interceptors*

In this section you'll see why services created using the `provide` method create some powerful opportunities.

4.4.1 *Why intercept?*

Imagine a scenario where you need to perform an action every time a remote service call is initiated, or possibly when it's returned. For instance, let's say that you have an authorization token you need to dynamically add to your endpoint URL as a URL parameter. You could go through and modify every single model to update the URL accordingly, but that could get tedious if you have a large number of services. Wouldn't it be nice if you could just set that in once for all outgoing calls? Wouldn't it be nice to be able to intercept any incoming or outgoing service call and perform some logic in one single place?

Using $httpProvider, you can create your own interceptors and make them available by pushing them into the $httpProvider.interceptors array. There are four types of interceptors that you can use: request, requestError, response, and responseError.

> **ON A PRACTICAL NOTE**   This is by no means a comprehensive discussion of interceptors. We'll focus on a practical example that exists in Angello to get your feet wet. If you want to learn more about interceptors, please check out the documentation at https://docs.angularjs.org/api/ng/service/$http.

4.4.2   *Interceptors in action*

You'll learn how to use an interceptor to trigger a loading indicator when there's an outgoing server call and to turn it off when the call is completed.

The first thing we need to do is to create our interceptor. We'll call it loading-Interceptor and inject the LoadingService into it:

```
// client/src/angello/Angello.js
myModule.factory('loadingInterceptor', function (LoadingService) {
    var loadingInterceptor = {
        request: function (config) {
            LoadingService.setLoading(true);
            return config;
        },
        response: function (response) {
            LoadingService.setLoading(false);
            return response;
        }
    };
    return loadingInterceptor;
});
```

We want to intercept the request and response calls, and so we need to define methods for each of those interceptors on our loadingInterceptor factory object. We're not going to do anything with the config and response parameters, but we need to make sure to return them so that the actual handlers have access to them. And within the request and response methods, we call LoadingService.setLoading(true) and LoadingService.setLoading(false) to turn the loading indicator on and off, respectively.

Now that our interceptor has been created, we need to make it available by pushing it into the $httpProvider.interceptors array:

```
// client/src/angello/Angello.js
myModule.config(function ($routeProvider, $httpProvider) {
    //...

    // Interceptor
    $httpProvider.interceptors.push('loadingInterceptor');

    //...
});
```

In the `myModule.config` block, we need to inject the `$httpProvider` so that it's available for us to push into the interceptors array. And once it's available, the mission is accomplished with this single line of code: `$httpProvider.interceptors.push ('loadingInterceptor')`.

This example is fairly simple, but by showing the pattern of how to set up an interceptor, we've opened the door to all kinds of possibilities.

4.5 Service decorators

The wonderful (and scary) thing about JavaScript is that it's dynamic and can be modified at the lowest levels to behave in a totally custom manner. This means that you can take an existing service and "decorate" it to enhance its functionality or change its behavior entirely. Let the monkey patching begin!

4.5.1 Why decorate?

In all seriousness, there are often real reasons to enhance an existing service to make it behave in a way that better suits your needs. Fixed languages are in a sense broken, because they force you to write thousands of lines of code to work around and provide functionality you wish you had right out of the box. This is where JavaScript and AngularJS excel, because they allow you to extend your imperative logic and declarative markup to do whatever you need.

To prove this point, we'll show in the next section how to enhance the `$log` service to provide better output to the console.

4.5.2 Enhanced logging

In the following section you'll learn how to decorate the `$log` service to prepend a timestamp to every `$log.debug` call that you make.

ENHANCING ANGULARJS LOGGING USING DECORATORS   I (Lukas) learned this technique from my good friend and mentor, Thomas Burleson. We'll cover just the rudimentary pieces of enhancing the logging service, but if you want to learn more please check out Thomas's excellent post at http://solutionoptimist .com/2013/10/07/.

The first thing we need to do is inject the `$provide` service into the config block of Angello. From here we can register our service decorator using `$provide.decorator`. This method takes two parameters: the name of the service we're decorating and the decorator function. The `$delegate` parameter to the decorator function is a reference to the original service we're decorating:

```
// client/src/angello/Angello.js
myModule.config(function ($routeProvider, $httpProvider, $provide) {     ⟵────┐
    //...

    // Decorator
```

**We inject $provide into
myModule.config so we can
use it to decorate $log.**

```
        $provide.decorator('$log', function ($delegate) {
            //...
            return $delegate;
        });
    });
```

We call $provide.decorator and pass in $log as the first parameter and our decorator as the second parameter.

Because $delegate represents the $log service in this case, we need to return it so it's available to the rest of the application. This will become extremely important once we decorate it.

And now that we have nuts and bolts in place, it's time to decorate!

This is a simple timestamp function that we'll use to output a pretty timestamp string. Check out the source code for the entire function.

```
// client/src/angello/Angello.js
myModule.config(function ($routeProvider, $httpProvider, $provide) {
    //...

    // Decorator
    $provide.decorator('$log', function ($delegate) {
        function timeStamp() {
            //...
        }

        // Save the original $log.debug()
        var debugFn = $delegate.debug;

        $delegate.debug = function () {
            // Prepend timestamp
            arguments[0] = timeStamp() + ' - ' + arguments[0];

            // Call the original with the output
        ➥    prepended with formatted timestamp
            debugFn.apply(null, arguments)
        };

        return $delegate;
    });
});
```

We store a reference to the original debug method so we can call apply on it later.

We overwrite the $log.debug with a new, decorated function.

We take the first argument to the method call and prepend the timestamp to it.

Finally, we call apply on the original debug function with the decorated arguments.

And now we can continue to call $log.debug as we before:

```
// client/src/angello/storyboard/controllers/StoryboardController.js
storyboard.getStories = function () {
    StoriesModel.all()
        .then(function (result) {
            storyboard.stories = (result !== 'null') ? result : {};
            $log.debug('RESULT', result);
        }, function (reason) {
            $log.debug('REASON', reason);
        });
};
```

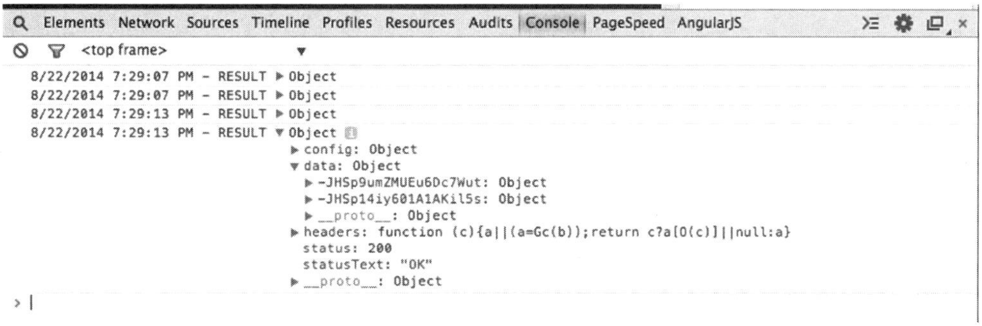

Figure 4.3   Console with decorated output

But the output we get is a little more interesting than before, as shown in figure 4.3.

4.6   *Testing consideration*

As always, we want to test our code to ensure quality and scalability. Let's dive into a couple scenarios that involve testing services.

4.6.1   *Testing a service*

We'll start by testing a simple service that performs a simple unit of logic. The perfect candidate for this task is the LoadingService, because its primary job is to control a property on $rootScope.

We'll start the test by declaring two variables called $rootScope and LoadingService that we'll assign the actual $rootScope and LoadingService to so that they're available for the entire spec:

```
// client/tests/specs/services/LoadingService.spec.js
describe('Loading Service', function () {
    var $rootScope, LoadingService;

    beforeEach(module('Angello.Common'));

    //...
});
```

We'll then load the Angello.Common module configuration code by calling module('Angello.Common') in the first beforeEach call. From there, we inject the $rootScope and LoadingService references into our spec and assign them to our local variables:

```
describe('Loading Service', function () {
    var $rootScope, LoadingService;

    beforeEach(module('Angello.Common'));

    beforeEach(inject(function (_$rootScope_, _LoadingService_) {
```

```
        $rootScope = _$rootScope_;
        LoadingService = _LoadingService_;
    }));

    //...
});
```

Note that we actually inject `_$rootScope_` and `_LoadingService_` as parameters. This is called *underscore wrapping* and is done so that we can assign those variables to the actual service name in our code. The `inject` method knows to strip out the underscores and return the actual service.

And now that we have a reference to `$rootScope` and `LoadingService`, we can call `LoadingService.setLoading` and test the result. What is the result of calling `LoadingService.setLoading`? Whatever parameter we pass into the method is what `$rootScope.loadingView` will be set to, and we can set up our assertions appropriately:

```
// client/tests/specs/services/LoadingService.spec.js
describe('Loading Service', function () {
    var $rootScope, LoadingService;

    beforeEach(module('Angello.Common'));

    beforeEach(inject(function (_$rootScope_, _LoadingService_) {
        $rootScope = _$rootScope_;
        LoadingService = _LoadingService_;
    }));

    it('should update $rootScope to false when setLoading is set to false',
        function () {
            LoadingService.setLoading(false);
            expect($rootScope.loadingView).toEqual(false);
    });

    it('should update $rootScope to true when setLoading is set to true',
        function () {
            LoadingService.setLoading(true);
            expect($rootScope.loadingView).toEqual(true);
    });
});
```

And now that we've walked through a spec for a simple service, let's take this a step further by writing a spec for a model that actually makes `$http` calls to a remote server.

4.6.2   *Using $httpBackend to mock server calls*

When writing tests for anything, it's important to stay focused on what you're actually testing. In the case of writing a spec for a model that makes remote server calls, it's important to understand that you're testing the logic in the model and not the results returned from the server or the ability of the `$http` service to do its job.

We'll test `StoriesModel`, and the first questions we need to ask are *What logic is happening in the service?* and *How do we test that?* Because we've implemented the model to be stateless, the only real logic we have to test is whether the URLs are being generated correctly to hit the right resource. We'll use `$httpBackend` to mock out specific server calls and then verify that `StoriesModel` did indeed hit our mock endpoints.

We can verify this in an `afterEach` block and by calling `verifyNoOutstanding-Expectation` and `verifyNoOutstandingRequest` on `$httpBackend`. This essentially asserts that `$httpBackend` was able to satisfy the request.

```
// client/tests/specs/services/StoriesModel.spec.js
describe('Stories Model', function () {

    //...

    afterEach(inject(function($httpBackend) {
        $httpBackend.verifyNoOutstandingExpectation();
        $httpBackend.verifyNoOutstandingRequest();
    }));

    //...
});
```

And just like that, we're ready to test! We'll examine the structure of one test to establish the pattern and then just point out the differences between the remaining tests. We'll test `StoriesModel.all`, so the first thing we need to do is to set up `$httpBackend` to handle the response:

```
describe('Stories Model', function () {
    //...

    it('Should get all', inject(function(StoriesModel, $httpBackend,
      $rootScope) {
        var response = [];
        $httpBackend.when(
            'GET', 'https://angello-angularjs.firebaseio
            .com/clients/1/stories/.json'
        ).respond(response);

        $rootScope.$broadcast('onCurrentUserId', 1);

        var promise = StoriesModel.all();
        $httpBackend.flush();

        promise.then(function(result) {
            expect(result).toEqual(response);
        });
        $rootScope.$digest();
    }));

    //...
});
```

Create a variable to store our response to use for comparison later.

Define the endpoint call we want to mock out and the response we want to return.

Call StoriesModel.all() and store the result.

Call $httpBackend.flush to trigger the trained response.

Assert that the result of the call is the same as the response we stored earlier.

Define the response in the then method of the promise.

Call $rootScope.$digest to trigger the promise.

The remaining tests are simply variations of the same pattern. We only have to change the `$httpBackend` response and call the `StoriesModel` method we want with the appropriate parameters.

GET ALL STORIES

```
$httpBackend.when(
  'GET', 'https://angello-angularjs.firebaseio.com/clients/1/stories/.json'
).respond(response);
var promise = StoriesModel.all();
```

CREATE A STORY

```
$httpBackend.when(
  'POST', 'https://angello-angularjs.firebaseio.com/clients/1/stories/.json'
).respond(response);
var promise = StoriesModel.create({});
```

GET A STORY

```
$httpBackend.when(
  'GET', 'https://angello-angularjs.firebaseio.com/clients/1/stories/1.json'
).respond(response);
var promise = StoriesModel.fetch(1);
```

UPDATE A STORY

```
$httpBackend.when(
  'PUT', 'https://angello-angularjs.firebaseio.com/clients/1/stories/1.json'
).respond(response);
var promise = StoriesModel.update(1, {});
```

DELETE A STORY

```
$httpBackend.when('DELETE',
    'https://angello-angularjs.firebaseio.com/clients/1/stories/1.json'
).respond(response);
var promise = StoriesModel.destroy(1);
```

4.6.3   *Best practices*

The best practice when unit testing services, as with anything, is to keep your tests focused on the item you're testing. Testing actual calls to the server or the `$http` service itself is unnecessary, as `$http` has it own set of tests, and integration tests are better suited for testing actual service calls.

Another technique worth mentioning is that you can manually resolve a promise by kicking off a digest cycle via `$rootScope.$digest`.

4.7   *Summary*

We've covered an incredible amount of ground in this chapter, and for that we congratulate you! We've laid the foundation for you to take these techniques and apply them to your own work in interesting ways. As with anything, AngularJS is not so much a collection of really complex topics, but a composition of rather fundamental techniques used in appropriate and clever ways.

Let's take a moment to review what we've covered in this chapter before moving on to the next chapter:

- Services are a way to define functionality that's common to the entire application.
- There are five types of services that you can define using the module convenience methods: `module.constant`, `module.value`, `module.service`, `module.factory`, and `module.provider`.
- Communication with remote servers is facilitated with the `$http` service, which has shortcut methods built into it that mirror REST verbs.
- The `$http` service is based on a `deferred / promise` API that provides mechanisms for you to handle asynchronous calls to the server.
- Further control over asynchronous operations can be exerted by using a `deferred` object returned by calling `$q.deferred`.
- Calls made using `$http` can be intercepted by creating an interceptor and pushing it into the `$httpProvider.interceptors` array during the `module.config` block.
- Services can be enhanced by capturing them in a `$provide.decorator` call in the `module.config` block and modifying its behavior.
- `$httpBackend` is great for mocking out server-side calls and defining the response.
- Manually resolve a promise in a unit test by calling `$rootScope.$digest`.

Directives 5

This chapter covers

- What directives are and why they're helpful
- Different kinds of directives and what they're best suited for
- The main components that make up a directive
- Some directives we use in Angello

5.1 Introduction to directives

Welcome to the world of directives: one of the most powerful and important features of the AngularJS framework. In this chapter we'll build three directives for Angello and discuss the techniques and reasoning behind each one. We'll start out simple and work our way up in complexity to some really neat things you can use in your own web applications.

5.1.1 What are directives?

AngularJS proclaims that it's "HTML enhanced for web apps!" What does it mean to *enhance* HTML?

HTML was born from a mentality rooted in print media, which was quite appropriate at the time. Browsers were limited, and the best you could hope for was to lay out content on a page much like you would a magazine or a newspaper. But fast-forward to the modern browser and HTML is incredibly limited and fixed when it comes to performing modern tasks like handling dynamic content, interactions, animations, and so on.

AngularJS solves this limitation by allowing you to define your own HTML behavior with directives. Directives are essentially custom HTML tags and attributes that you can create to do some very clever things. And by "clever," we mean "anything you want."

5.1.2 Why we need directives

HTML is a fixed language in the sense that you get what's on the spec and that's that. And because it's fixed, it's broken before you even get started. Countless developers have torn their hair out working around the limitations that HTML has imposed on them. Most of the time, workarounds involve augmenting HTML with other technologies like CSS and JavaScript.

So why do you need directives? For your sanity, that's why. All kidding aside, when you can find a way to elegantly extend HTML to overcome its limitations, you're in a position to write modern web applications without resorting to circus tricks.

5.1.3 Why we want directives

Setting aside the need to overcome the limitations of HTML for a moment, there's something elegant and artistic about writing code that's expressive and describes the domain you're in and the problems you're trying to solve. One outstanding feature of directives is that they allow you to turn your HTML into a domain-specific language.

We're building a project management board that tracks user stories. Wouldn't it be convenient if we had a tag called user-story that we could use in our markup? Would we have any question in our minds about what that tag did? That's the beauty of directives!

5.2 Directives 101: a quick foundation

We'll lay the foundation as to what generally goes into a directive so we can start building our own as quickly as possible (see figure 5.1). Directives generally have three parts in them—the controller function, the link function, and the *directive definition object* (DDO). A directive will always have a DDO but may only have a link or controller function depending on the context.

The DDO is the foundation of the directive. It tells AngularJS how the directive should be handled during the compilation cycle and what it should do. The DDO is where you can set things like how the directive's going to be marked up in the HTML, how its scope is going to interact with the outside world, and whether it's going to use the existing HTML or load new HTML into the directive.

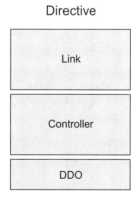

Figure 5.1 **When you condense directives into three main parts, things get much simpler.**

The controller function works just like controllers in the rest of your application. It's responsible for setting state for the directive and defining functionality for it as well. This is also where you would interact with a service if the directive needs to perform an action outside of its narrow area of focus.

The link function is where any DOM manipulation in your application goes. This is also where you put any initialization and interaction code for third-party plugins. For instance, we're going to integrate with a jQuery plugin in our second example, and the link function is where we initialize that plugin. It's also where you would capture any events emitted by a third-party plugin and process it for the rest of the AngularJS application.

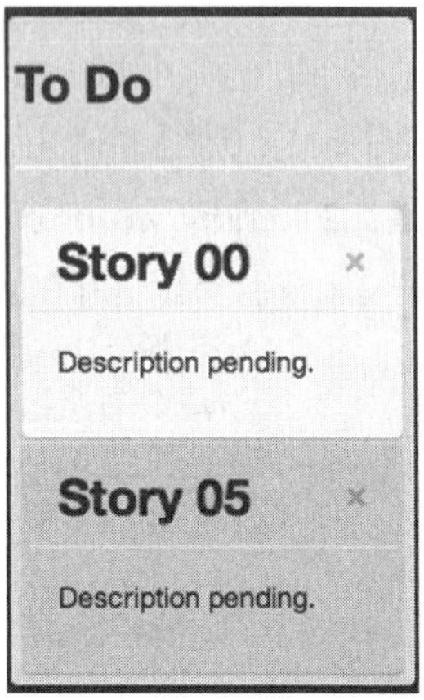

5.2.1   *The user story directive*

Our first directive will be a user story directive that's purposely simplistic so that you can get your feet wet with the basic structure of how a directive is put together—see figure 5.2.

Figure 5.2   The user story directive

CREATE THE DIRECTIVE

Defining a directive is very similar to defining a controller or service, in that you give it a name and a factory function that will return an object of a defined sort when the directive is needed. Following is the basic syntax for creating a controller. Notice that you give it a name as the first parameter of the controller method call and then a factory function as the second parameter:

```
myModule.controller('MainCtrl', function ($scope) {
  // ...
});
```

When you define a directive, the pattern is the same. We'll give this directive a name of userstory, and then we'll start to build out the factory function as we progress:

```
myModule.directive('userstory', function () {
  // ...
});
```

Now let's fill out the directive with a link function, a controller function, and a definition object to lay the foundation for the rest of the functionality in the directive. Notice that we also have a controllerAs attribute on the definition object so we can reference the controller everywhere in the template:

```
// client/src/angello/user/directives/UserStoryDirective.js
angular.module('Angello.User')
    .directive('userstory',
        function () {
            var linker = function (scope, element, attrs) {
                // Pending
            };
            var controller = function ($scope) {
```

```
            // Pending
        };
        return {
            restrict: 'A',
            controller: controller,
            controllerAs: 'userStory',
            link: linker
        };
    });
```

THE DIRECTIVE DEFINITION OBJECT

The definition object is just an extension of the module pattern where you return an object to be instantiated during an AngularJS compilation cycle. The difference is that a specific API is available to tell AngularJS exactly how the directive should behave. In the preceding example, we stated that we want to restrict the directive to only be used as an attribute, as noted by the line `restrict: 'A'`. Then we indicated that we want to use the `linker` function and `controller` function as the link and controller functions, respectively.

AngularJS is incredibly powerful, with almost infinite possibilities of what you can do, but the 80/20 rule definitely applies. Nowhere is this more true than in the case of directives. There are some pretty exotic options you can invoke from the definition object, but they're generally relegated to edge cases and rarely seen in the wild. For the sake of space and sanity, we'll endeavor to stay within the confines of what's reasonably useful.

THE LINK FUNCTION

Remember when we talked about the link function being the primary place to do DOM manipulation? Everything you need to accomplish this is delivered to you via an AngularJS care package in the form of the function parameters. The `scope` parameter is simply the scope of the current instantiation of the directive you're working with. It's worth mentioning that this is the same scope object as the `$scope` parameter in the controller function. The `element` parameter is the element that the directive is declared on, but wrapped in a jQuery object. The `attrs` parameter is an array of all of the attributes on the element that the directive was declared on.

> **JQUERY** AngularJS ships with a subset of jQuery out of the box, but if you've included jQuery in your project, then AngularJS defers to that instance

THE CONTROLLER FUNCTION

The controller function works almost exactly like a controller you'd define on your application. Just as you want to segment DOM manipulation to the link function, you want to keep imperative logic in the controller. Because the link function and the controller function share the same scope object, it's not uncommon to call a function in the controller from the link function. The only difference worth noting is that services are injected into the directive and are then available to the controller as opposed to injecting services into stand-alone controllers directly.

USE THE DIRECTIVE

Now that we have the skeleton of our user story directive in place, let's go ahead and actually use the directive in our markup.

This is the HTML that visually represents the user story currently:

```html
<!-- client/src/angello/storyboard/tmpl/storyboard.html -->
<li ng-repeat="story in storyboard.stories | filter:{status:status.name}"
    class="story"
    ng-click="storyboard.setCurrentStory(story)">

    <article>
        <div>
            <button type="button" class="close"
                    ng-click="userStory.deleteStoryBoard(story.id)">
                x
            </button>
            <p class="title">{{story.title}}</p>
        </div>
        <div class="type-bar {{story.type}}"></div>
        <div>
            <p>{{story.description}}</p>
        </div>
    </article>
</li>
```

This is the same HTML with the userstory directive defined on it:

```html
// client/src/angello/storyboard/tmpl/storyboard.html
<li userstory
    ng-repeat="story in storyboard.stories | filter:{status:status.name}"
    class="story"
    ng-click="storyboard.setCurrentStory(story)">

    <article>
        <div>
            <button type="button" class="close"
                    ng-click="userStory.deleteStoryBoard(story.id)">
                x
            </button>
            <p class="title">{{story.title}}</p>
        </div>
        <div class="type-bar {{story.type}}"></div>
        <div>
            <p>{{story.description}}</p>
        </div>
    </article>
</li>
```

Notice the difference. A single attribute. Without turning into a cheerleader, being able to extend the user story HTML to include all of the extra functionality we're going to define in a single attribute is a really powerful feature!

ADD DOM EVENT HANDLERS TO THE DIRECTIVE LINK FUNCTION

Speaking of functionality, let's actually do something with the directive. We'll start with the link function and add a slight fade when the user mouses over the user story, and then restore it when the user mouses out.

If you go to the jQuery website and look up the .mouseover() function, you'll see a snippet of code that looks like this:

```
$('#outer').mouseover(function() {
  $('#log').append('<div>Handler for .mouseover() called.</div>');
});
```

We'll do something similar, but you'll soon see that the task is actually much easier within the link function:

```
// client/src/angello/user/directives/UserStoryDirective.js
angular.module('Angello.User')
    .directive('userstory',
        function () {
            var linker = function (scope, element, attrs) {
                element
                    .mouseover(function () {
                      element.css({ 'opacity': 0.9 });
                    })
                    .mouseout(function () {
                      element.css({ 'opacity': 1.0 })
                    });
            };
            var controller = function ($scope) {
                // Pending
            };
            return {
                restrict: 'A',
                controller: controller,
                controllerAs: 'userStory',
                link: linker
            };
        });
```

Because the element object is already a jQuery wrapped object, you can attach the event handler directly to the element object without having to query the DOM. You also don't have to worry about the DOM element being ready, since the directive doesn't fire until the element has been added to the page and the compilation cycle has run. It is like a premium valet service just for your DOM!

With that said, we chain two events together like this,

```
element.mouseover(function () {
  // ...
}).mouseout(function () {
  // ...
});
```

and then set the opacity in the event handler.

CREATE A DELETE STORY METHOD ON ANGELLOMODEL

Let's shift gears and add the ability to delete a story by clicking the Delete button on the user story, that is, the X in the top right-hand corner of the Summary box.

Practically speaking, an object shouldn't be responsible for moving itself from the collection that it lives in. We need to inject StoriesModel to accommodate this functionality, since it owns all of the stories for the application. We'll also use the $rootScope and $log services in a callback function:

```
// client/src/angello/user/directives/UserStoryDirective.js
angular.module('Angello.User')
    .directive('userstory',
        function ($rootScope, StoriesModel, $log) {

            //...

        });
```

CREATE A DELETE STORY METHOD ON THE DIRECTIVE CONTROLLER

Now we need to create a deleteStory method and make it available to the directive. This is simply a matter of adding a deleteStory method on the reference to the $scope object (userStory), and from there calling the destroy method on Stories-Model and passing the id parameter to it. We no longer need to pass the $scope object into the controller, since we assign a reference to the this keyword:

```
// client/src/angello/user/directives/UserStoryDirective.js
angular.module('Angello.User')
    .directive('userstory',
        function ($rootScope, StoriesModel, $log) {
            //...
            var controller = function () {
                var userStory = this;
                userStory.deleteStory = function (id) {
                    StoriesModel.destroy(id)
                        .then(function (result) {
                            $rootScope.$broadcast('storyDeleted');
                            $log.debug('RESULT', result);
                        }, function (reason) {
                            $log.debug('ERROR', reason);
                        });
                };
            };
            return {
                //...
                controller: controller,
            };
        });
```

In the same fashion as StoryboardCtrl, we call the destroy method on the Stories-Model service and use .then to execute success and error functions. All the $rootScope.$broadcast does is alert the StorboardCtrl about the deletion so that it can update the stories collection and reset the form.

ADD A BUTTON TO CALL DELETESTORY ON CLICK

The last thing we need to do is write up the deleteStory method on userStory to the actual view. This is familiar territory, as we add a button with ng-click defined to call deleteStory and pass story.id in as the parameter:

```
<!-- client/src/angello/storyboard/tmpl/storyboard.html -->
<li userstory
    ng-repeat="story in storyboard.stories | filter:{status:status.name}"
    class="story"
    ng-click="storyboard.setCurrentStory(story)">
    <article class="{{story.type}}">
        <div>
            <button type="button" class="close"
                ng-click="deleteStory(story.id)">
                x
            </button>
            <p class="title">{{story.title}}</p>
        </div>
        <div class="type-bar {{story.type}}"></div>
        <div>
            <p>{{story.description}}</p>
        </div>
    </article>
</li>
```

Hooray! The user story directive is done. Time for a quick review before we move on:

- We defined a directive, including the three main parts: link function, controller function, and definition object.
- We explored the parameters of the link function and why they make DOM manipulation so breezy.
- We talked about how a controller function works pretty much like an application controller, but shares $scope with the link function.
- We showed how the directive definition object is used to define the directive, and more importantly, that the 80/20 rule definitely applies here.

Onward and upward!

5.3 *A more advanced feature*

So being able to fade HTML on mouseover is a good start, but how about something more ambitious? We've got it. We'll flex our DOM muscles and create *three* directives that allow the user to drag a user story from one status column to another—see figure 5.3.

5.3.1 *The drag-and-drop feature*

The three directives that comprise our drag-and-drop feature are drag-container, drop-container, and drop-target. In a nutshell, the drag-container is the element we drag, drop-container is the element where a drag-container will be dropped, and drop-target decides which area inside the drop-container the drag-container

Figure 5.3 The drag-and-drop feature

should be dropped into. We'll also create a service so we can share data between the drag-container and drop-container directives. We'll call this service $dragging.

CREATE THE FILE

Before we get started, let's create a file called DragAndDrop.js and put it in client/src/angello/storyboard/directives. Don't forget to add it to boot.js!

```
// client/assets/js/boot.js
{ file: 'src/angello/storyboard/directives/DragAndDrop.js' },
```

CREATE THE DRAG-CONTAINER DIRECTIVE

The first piece of the puzzle is creating a draggable container. We follow the same pattern as before: declare the directive with the name dragContainer and a factory function that has a link function and a definition object:

```
// client/src/angello/storyboard/directives/DragAndDrop.js
angular.module('Angello.Storyboard')
    .directive('dragContainer', function () {
        return {
            restrict: 'A',
            controller: 'DragContainerController',
            controllerAs: 'dragContainer',
            link: function ($scope, $element, $attrs, dragContainer) {
                dragContainer.init($element);

                $element.on('dragstart',
                ➥    dragContainer.handleDragStart.bind(dragContainer));
                $element.on('dragend',
                ➥    dragContainer.handleDragEnd.bind(dragContainer));

                $scope.$watch($attrs.dragContainer,
                ➥    dragContainer.updateDragData.bind(dragContainer));
                $attrs.$observe('mimeType',
                ➥    dragContainer.updateDragType.bind(dragContainer));
```

```
                    $attrs.$set('draggable', true);
            }
        };
    })

    .controller('DragContainerController', function ($dragging) {
    });
```

NOTE We actually define the link function inline, and we define the controller function outside of the directive entirely this time. This is just semantics; you can do it whatever way suits you.

Let's take a look at the link function. We define it with four parameters: $scope, $element, $attrs, and dragContainer. You've already seen the first three parameters in action; the fourth parameter is actually a reference to the DragContainer-Controller. We reference the controller using the same name as the controllerAs property on the DDO for consistency.

Our first order of action is to call the init method on the DragContainer-Controller and pass in the current directive's element. Don't worry; we'll dive into DragContainerController's methods in a minute.

Because $element is just a jQuery-wrapped DOM element, we can listen for browser events on it. Yes, HTML5 has native dragging events! We want to listen for the dragstart and dragend events and then invoke the appropriate controller callbacks. The bind method appended to both of the callbacks essentially makes sure that they're called within the context of the DragContainerController, or that the this keyword refers to DragContainerController, not the link function in which it was called.

Next, we use $scope.$watch to listen for changes to $attrs.dragContainer. As you'll see, $attrs.dragContainer is assigned to the story data model, and any time that data changes, we want to call updateDragData on the controller.

Now we want to listen for changes to the mimeType attribute and trigger the updateDragType on the controller. We use $observe instead of $watch because the value we're watching is evaluated as text, not an actual Angular expression.

Lastly, when everything is initialized, we set the draggable attribute on our directive to true. We do this so the browser knows that this element is draggable.

5.3.2 *Use the drag-container directive*

Now that we've created the drag-container directive, let's add it to our HTML:

```html
<!-- client/src/angello/storyboard/tmpl/storyboard.html -->
<li userstory
    ng-repeat="story in storyboard.stories | filter: {status:status.name}"
    drag-container="story" mime-type="application/x-angello-status"
    class="story my-repeat-animation"
    ng-click="storyboard.setCurrentStory(story)">
```

We define the drag-container directive on the same li as our userstory directive. We then assign it the data model we want to use, in this case story, and define a mime-type attribute as `application/x-angello-status`. This could be any value, as long as the `drop-container` directive has an `accepts` attribute with a value (or array of values) that contains the `mime-type` value.

5.3.3   *Build the controller*

Now that we've created the directive and placed it in the HTML, let's go ahead and build out the controller:

```
// client/src/angello/storyboard/directives/DragAndDrop.js
angular.module('Angello.Storyboard')
    .controller('DragContainerController', function ($dragging) {
        var dragContainer = this;

        dragContainer.init = function (el) {
            dragContainer.el = el;
        };
    });
```

First, as always, we create a top-level reference to `this` for use later in our controller. We then define an init function that takes the element from the link function and assigns it to the controller so we have access to it:

```
// client/src/angello/storyboard/directives/DragAndDrop.js
angular.module('Angello.Storyboard')
    .controller('DragContainerController', function ($dragging) {

        //...

        dragContainer.handleDragStart = function (e) {
            if (e.originalEvent) e = e.originalEvent;

            e.dataTransfer.dropEffect = 'move';
            e.dataTransfer.effectAllowed = 'move';

            dragContainer.el.addClass('drag-container-active');
            dragContainer.dragging = true;

            $dragging.setData(dragContainer.data);
            $dragging.setType(dragContainer.type);
        };
    });
```

If `e.originalEvent` exists, we assign it back to `e`. We then set the `effectAllowed` and `dropEffect` properties on the `e.dataTransfer` object. These let the browser know which effects are allowed and what kind of visual effect to use on the element when dropped, respectively.

Then we add a class, set the `dragging` property on the controller to true, and set `data` and `type` on the `$dragging` service:

```
// client/src/angello/storyboard/directives/DragAndDrop.js
angular.module('Angello.Storyboard')
    .controller('DragContainerController', function ($dragging) {
```

```
//...

dragContainer.handleDragEnd = function (e) {
    if (e.originalEvent) e = e.originalEvent;

    angular.element(e.target).removeClass('drag-active');

    dragContainer.el.removeClass('drag-container-active');
    dragContainer.dragging = false;

    $dragging.setData(null);
    $dragging.setType(null);
    };
});
```

Here we assign the originalEvent to e, remove a couple of classes, set the dragging property on the controller to false, and set both properties in the $dragging service to null.

```
// client/src/angello/storyboard/directives/DragAndDrop.js
angular.module('Angello.Storyboard')
    .controller('DragContainerController', function ($dragging) {

        //...

        dragContainer.updateDragData = function (data) {
            dragContainer.data = data;

            if (dragContainer.dragging)
        ➥       $dragging.setData(dragContainer.data);


        };
    });
```

We assign the passed-in data to the controller and then, if the dragging property on the controller is true (or the element is still being dragged), we update the data property on the $dragging service:

```
// client/src/angello/storyboard/directives/DragAndDrop.js
angular.module('Angello.Storyboard')
    .controller('DragContainerController', function ($dragging) {

        //...

        dragContainer.updateDragType = function (type) {
            dragContainer.type = type || 'text/x-drag-and-drop';

            if (dragContainer.dragging)
        ➥       $dragging.setType(dragContainer.type);
        };
    });
```

We initialize the type property on the controller to the type parameter if it exists, and to text/x-drag-and-drop if it doesn't. Then, if the element is still being dragged, we update the type property on the $dragging service.

5.3.4   *Create the drop-container directive*

Next, we need a container that can receive our drag-container directive when the drag-container is dragged over it. Naturally, we call it drop-container:

```
// client/src/angello/storyboard/directives/DragAndDrop.js
angular.module('Angello.Storyboard')
    .directive('dropContainer', function ($document, $parse) {
        return {
            restrict: 'A',
            controller: 'DropContainerController',
            controllerAs: 'dropContainer',
            link: function ($scope, $element, $attrs, dropContainer) {
                var bindTo = function (event) {
                    return function (e) {
                        return $scope.$apply(function () {
                            return dropContainer['handle' + event](e);
                        });
                    };
                };

                var dragEnd =
                    dropContainer.handleDragEnd.bind(dropContainer);
                var handleDragEnter = bindTo('DragEnter');
                var handleDragOver = bindTo('DragOver');
                var handleDragLeave = bindTo('DragLeave');
                var handleDrop = bindTo('Drop');

                dropContainer.init($element, $scope, {
                    onDragEnter: $parse($attrs.onDragEnter),
                    onDragOver: $parse($attrs.onDragOver),
                    onDragLeave: $parse($attrs.onDragLeave),
                    onDrop: $parse($attrs.onDrop),
                });

                $element.on('dragenter', handleDragEnter);
                $element.on('dragover', handleDragOver);
                $element.on('dragleave', handleDragLeave);
                $element.on('drop', handleDrop);

                $scope.$watch($attrs.accepts,
                    dropContainer.updateMimeTypes.bind(dropContainer));

                $document.on('dragend', dragEnd);

                $scope.$on('$destroy', function () {
                    $document.off('dragend', dragEnd);
                });
            }
        };
    });
```

We continue the pattern: a DDO with an inline link function that has four parameters, the fourth being a reference to the controller created outside of the directive.

In the link function, we create a `bindTo` method that takes an event name and turns it into a method that can respond to a DOM event with the appropriate controller method call *and*, which passes in the original DOM event. The `$scope.$apply` method takes an expression from outside the AngularJS framework (DOM events, XHR, and so on) and executes it within the context of the framework (triggers a `$digest` cycle so all the watchers are evaluated properly).

Then we create a reference to the controller's `handleDragEnd` function (again notice that we use `.bind` so that the method is executed in the context of the controller, not the link function). Then we use our freshly baked `bindTo` method to create four different callback methods that we'll use to respond to four different DOM events.

Next we call `init` on the `DropContainerController` and pass in three parameters: the jQuery-wrapped DOM element on which the directive was defined, the link function's scope, and a list of callbacks that the controller can access and execute. The `$parse` service takes an AngularJS expression from `$attrs` and converts it into a function so we can call it.

Hooray for simple jQuery! Now we listen for four different DOM events—dragenter, dragover, dragleave, and drop—and attach the appropriate controller methods as callbacks.

Moving right along, we listen for three different events. First, we watch the `accepts` attribute on the directive; every time `accepts` changes, we invoke the `updateMimeTypes` method on the controller. We then create a watcher on `$document` (which is equivalent to `window.document`) so that any time the `dragend` event is triggered, we invoke the controller's `dragEnd` method. Lastly, we create an AngularJS watcher that removes this handler whenever the `$destroy` event is triggered in Angular.

5.3.5 *Use the drop-container directive*

In the following code, we instantiate the `drop-container` directive by attaching it to the list items created by `ngRepeat`:

```
<!-- client/src/angello/storyboard/tmpl/storyboard.html -->
<li userstory
    ng-repeat="story in storyboard.stories | filter: {status:status.name}"
    drag-container="story" mime-type="application/x-angello-status"
    drop-container="" accepts="['application/x-angello-status']"
    class="story my-repeat-animation"
    ng-click="storyboard.setCurrentStory(story)">

<!-- ... -->

<div class="emptystatus" drop-container=""
    accepts="['application/x-angello- status']"
    on-drop="storyboard.finalizeDrop(data)"
    on-drag-enter="storyboard.changeStatus(data, status)"
    ng-if="storyboard.isEmptyStatus(status)">
</div>
```

Notice that we actually define the `drop-container` directive in two places: the user-story `li` and another div that represents the unoccupied area of each status column. We don't add the `on-drop` and `on-drag-enter` attributes to the `userstory` element because we're going to add `drop-target` directives as children of `userstory` and define those attributes there.

We define another attribute called `accepts` and assign it an array of MIME types that we can drag over it. In this case, we only need one value, `['application/x-angello-status']`, because there's only one type of element we need to drag.

Lastly, we pass the appropriate `StoryboardCtrl` callbacks to the `on-drop` and `on-drag-enter` attributes so that they can be invoked from the directive.

5.3.6   *Build the controller*

Buckle your seatbelts because we're about to dive into the unknown! Okay, that was a bit dramatic, but do pay extra attention; it'll be worth it.

```
// client/src/angello/storyboard/directives/DragAndDrop.js
angular.module('Angello.Storyboard')
    .controller('DropContainerController', function ($dragging) {
        var dropContainer = this;
        var targets = {};
        var validAnchors = 'center top top-right right
            bottom-right bottom bottom-left left top-left'.split(' ');

        dropContainer.init = function (el, scope, callbacks) {
            dropContainer.el = el;
            dropContainer.scope = scope;
            dropContainer.callbacks = callbacks;
            dropContainer.accepts = ['text/x-drag-and-drop'];

            dropContainer.el.addClass('drop-container');
        };
    });
```

We create a top-level reference to `this`, and we create two other variables: a `targets` object that will hold all of the available drop targets and a `validAnchors` array that holds all of the valid anchor types. We then create an `init` method that takes the `$element`, `$scope`, and `callbacks` arguments and assigns them to the controller so we can use them throughout. We also default the `accepts` attribute to `['text/x-drag-and-drop']` and add a `drop-container` class to the directive's element.

```
// client/src/angello/storyboard/directives/DragAndDrop.js
angular.module('Angello.Storyboard')
    .controller('DropContainerController', function ($dragging) {

        //...

        dropContainer.addDropTarget = function (anchor, dropTarget) {
            if (validAnchors.indexOf(anchor) < 0)
                throw new Error('Invalid anchor point ' + anchor);
            if (targets[anchor])
```

```
⮡    throw new Error('Duplicate drop targets for the anchor ' + anchor);

         targets[anchor] = dropTarget;
     };

     dropContainer.removeDropTarget = function (anchor) {
         if (targets[anchor] && targets[anchor] === anchor) {
             dropContainer.activeTarget = null;
         }

         delete targets[anchor];
     };
 });
```

Our next stop is the addDropTarget method. As you'll see, this method actually gets called from the drop-target directive. It takes an anchor and a reference to an instance of the drop-target directive; and if the anchor is not a valid anchor type or if a drop-target instance already exists for the provided anchor type, we throw the appropriate error. Otherwise, we set an attribute on the targets object whose key is the provided anchor and whose value is the drop-target instance.

Next, in the removeDropTarget method (which also gets called from the drop-target directive), we simply remove the drop-target instance at the provided anchor key in the targets object:

```
// client/src/angello/storyboard/directives/DragAndDrop.js
angular.module('Angello.Storyboard')
    .controller('DropContainerController', function ($dragging) {

        //...

        dropContainer.updateMimeTypes = function (mimeTypes) {
            if (!mimeTypes) mimeTypes = ['text/x-drag-and-drop'];
            if (!angular.isArray(mimeTypes)) mimeTypes = [mimeTypes];

            dropContainer.accepts = mimeTypes;
        };
    });
```

If the mimeTypes parameter is empty, we initialize it to an array with one value, text/x-drag-and-drop; similarly, if that same parameter is not an array, we go ahead and make it one. Then we assign it to the controller so we can use it later:

```
// client/src/angello/storyboard/directives/DragAndDrop.js
angular.module('Angello.Storyboard')
    .controller('DropContainerController', function ($dragging) {

        //...

        dropContainer.updateDragTarget = function (e, skipUpdateTarget) {
            if (e.originalEvent) e = e.originalEvent;

            var activeTarget = null;
            var activeAnchor = null;
            var minDistanceSq = Number.MAX_VALUE;
```

```
        var prevAnchor = dropContainer.activeAnchor;
        var prevTarget = dropContainer.activeTarget;

        if (!skipUpdateTarget) {
            angular.forEach(targets, function (dropTarget, anchor) {
                var width = dropContainer.el[0].offsetWidth;
                var height = dropContainer.el[0].offsetHeight;
                var anchorX = width / 2;
                var anchorY = height / 2;

                if (anchor.indexOf('left') >= 0) anchorX = 0;
                if (anchor.indexOf('top') >= 0) anchorY = 0;
                if (anchor.indexOf('right') >= 0) anchorX = width;
                if (anchor.indexOf('bottom') >= 0) anchorY = height;

                var distanceSq = Math.pow(anchorX - e.offsetX, 2)
                               + Math.pow(anchorY - e.offsetY, 2);

                if (distanceSq < minDistanceSq) {
                    activeAnchor = anchor;
                    activeTarget = dropTarget;
                    minDistanceSq = distanceSq;
                }
            });
        }

        dropContainer.activeAnchor = activeAnchor;
        dropContainer.activeTarget = activeTarget;

        var eventData = {
            $event: e,
            data: $dragging.getData(),
            anchor: activeAnchor,
            target: activeTarget,
            prevAnchor: prevAnchor,
            prevTarget: prevTarget
        };

        if (prevTarget !== activeTarget) {
            if (prevTarget) {
                dropContainer.el.
            ➡    removeClass('drop-container-active-' + prevAnchor);
                prevTarget.handleDragLeave(eventData);
            }

            if (activeTarget) {
                dropContainer.el.
            ➡    addClass('drop-container-active-' + activeAnchor);
                activeTarget.handleDragEnter(eventData);
            }
        }

        return eventData;
    };
});
});
```

Hold on to your seats; this is where it gets intense. We first assign the `e.original-Event` to `e`. Then we create the `activeTarget` and `activeAnchor` variables and initialize them to `null`, and create the `minDistanceSq` variable and assign it `Number.MAX_VALUE`. `Number.MAX_VALUE` represents the "maximum numeric value representable in JavaScript" (from https://developer.mozilla.org). Really, we just needed a large number that would never realistically be reached, so it was just another way of saying "a really big number."

We then define two more variables, `prevAnchor` and `prevTarget`, that hold references to `dropContainer.activeAnchor` and `dropContainer.activeTarget`.

There may be times when we don't want to update our `drop-target` instances. If we *do*, then we loop over each of the targets and perform some spatial logic. This consists of getting the current element's width and height, saving them, and then dividing both of those by two to initialize a couple of anchor points. At initialization, these two anchor points represent the "center" of the `drop-container` directive element. Now we check for keywords in the `anchor` parameter and update our anchor points accordingly.

You math majors get ready to party—we're going to use the Pythagorean Theorem! We get the mouse pointer's distance from `anchorX` and the mouse pointer's distance from `anchorY` by subtracting `e.offsetX` and `e.offsetY` from them, respectively. Then we square both these values and add them together. The result is the square of the distance between the mouse pointer and the position represented by the two anchor points. Then, if that distance is less than `minDistanceSq`, we set the current anchor and current target, and update `minDistanceSq` to the `distanceSq` we just evaluated.

Then we update the `activeAnchor` and `activeTarget` properties on the controller to the latest values.

Next, we define an `eventData` object and populate it with the current event, data from the `$dragging` service, the current anchor, current target, previous anchor, and previous target.

Now, if the previous target and the current target are different *and* there *was* a previous target, we remove the appropriate class and call the `handleDragLeave` method on the previous target, passing in our newly formed `eventData`. If there is a current target, we add the appropriate class to it and call the `handleDragEnter` method on it, passing in the `eventData`.

Finally, we return the `eventData`. Whew!

```
// client/src/angello/storyboard/directives/DragAndDrop.js
angular.module('Angello.Storyboard')
    .controller('DropContainerController', function ($dragging) {

        //...

        dropContainer.handleDragEnter = function (e) {
            if (e.originalEvent) e = e.originalEvent;

            if (!dropContainer.accepts
                || dropContainer.accepts.indexOf($dragging.getType()) >= 0) {
```

```
            e.preventDefault();
        } else {
            return;
        }

        var eventData = dropContainer.updateDragTarget(e);

        dropContainer.el.children().css({'pointer-events': 'none'});
        dropContainer.el.addClass('drop-container-active');

        if (dropContainer.callbacks.onDragEnter) {
            dropContainer.callbacks
    ➡        .onDragEnter(dropContainer.scope, eventData);
        }
    };
});
```

As usual, we want the original event. If the accepts property on the controller is not defined *or* if the current type in the $dragging service is included in the list of types in the accepts array, then we prevent the default DOM actions from occurring and proceed with the rest of the method. We have to prevent the default action if we want to implement our own functionality. If we don't, the drop-container won't react to the dragenter event.

Then we call the updateDragTarget method, pass in the current event, and assign the variable eventData to the return value of that call. Also, we get rid of pointer events on the drop-container element's children and add a class to that same element.

Lastly, we invoke the proper callback if it exists and pass in the current scope and the eventData object:

```
// client/src/angello/storyboard/directives/DragAndDrop.js
angular.module('Angello.Storyboard')
    .controller('DropContainerController', function ($dragging) {

        //...

        dropContainer.handleDragOver = function (e) {
            if (e.originalEvent) e = e.originalEvent;

            if (!dropContainer.accepts
            || dropContainer.accepts.indexOf($dragging.getType()) >= 0) {
                e.preventDefault();
            } else {
                return;
            }

            var eventData = dropContainer.updateDragTarget(e);

            if (eventData.target) {
                eventData.target.handleDragOver(eventData);
            }

            if (dropContainer.callbacks.onDragOver) {
```

```
            dropContainer.callbacks
        ➥        .onDragOver(dropContainer.scope, eventData);
            }
        };
    });
```

Once again, we grab the original event, proceed if we have the right mime-type, and call updateDragTarget to get the event data. If eventData has a target, we call that target's handleDragOver method (the handleDragOver method defined on the DropTargetController). Then, if an onDragOver callback has been defined on the controller, we call it and pass in the current scope and eventData.

```
// client/src/angello/storyboard/directives/DragAndDrop.js
angular.module('Angello.Storyboard')
    .controller('DropContainerController', function ($dragging) {

        //...

        dropContainer.handleDragLeave = function (e) {
            if (e.originalEvent) e = e.originalEvent;

            var eventData = dropContainer.updateDragTarget(e, true);

            dropContainer.el.children().css({'pointer-events': null});
            dropContainer.el.removeClass('drop-container-active');

            if (dropContainer.callbacks.onDragLeave) {
                dropContainer.callbacks
        ➥        .onDragLeave(dropContainer.scope, eventData);
            }
        };
    });
```

You probably have noticed the pattern by now. The only difference here is that we reset the pointer-events rule on the drop-container element's children to null and remove a class from the element:

```
// client/src/angello/storyboard/directives/DragAndDrop.js
angular.module('Angello.Storyboard')
    .controller('DropContainerController', function ($dragging) {

        //…

        dropContainer.handleDragEnd = function (e) {

            dropContainer.el.children().css({'pointer-events': null});
            dropContainer.el.removeClass('drop-container-active');
        };
    });
```

Again, we reset the pointer-events rule on the element's children to null and remove a class from the element:

```javascript
// client/src/angello/storyboard/directives/DragAndDrop.js
angular.module('Angello.Storyboard')
    .controller('DropContainerController', function ($dragging) {

        //…

        dropContainer.handleDrop = function (e) {
            if (e.originalEvent) e = e.originalEvent;

            if (!dropContainer.accepts
                || dropContainer.accepts.indexOf($dragging.getType()) >= 0) {
                e.preventDefault();
            } else {
                return;
            }

            var eventData = dropContainer.updateDragTarget(e);

            if (eventData.target) {
                eventData.target.handleDrop(eventData);
            }

            if (dropContainer.callbacks.onDrop) {
                dropContainer.callbacks
            ➥      .onDrop(dropContainer.scope, eventData);
            }

            dropContainer.handleDragEnd(e);
        };
    });
```

The handleDrop method is nearly identical to the handleDragOver method. We only need to change the method called on eventData.target to handleDrop, update the controller callback method to onDrop, and call the handleDragEnd method defined on the controller.

5.3.7　Create the drop-target directive

The drop-container can use nested drop-target directives to delegate the region of the drop-container in which the drag-container gets dropped. Here's what that drop-target directive looks like:

```javascript
// client/src/angello/storyboard/directives/DragAndDrop.js
angular.module('Angello.Storyboard')
    .directive('dropTarget', function ($parse) {
        return {
            restrict: 'A',
            require: ['^dropContainer', 'dropTarget'],
            controller: 'DropTargetController',
            controllerAs: 'dropTarget',
            link: function ($scope, $element, $attrs, ctrls) {
                var dropContainer = ctrls[0];
                var dropTarget = ctrls[1];
                var anchor = $attrs.dropTarget || 'center';
```

```
            var destroy =
➡           dropContainer.removeDropTarget.bind(dropContainer, anchor);

            $element.addClass('drop-target drop-target-' + anchor);

            dropTarget.init($element, $scope, {
                onDragEnter: $parse($attrs.onDragEnter),
                onDragOver: $parse($attrs.onDragOver),
                onDragLeave: $parse($attrs.onDragLeave),
                onDrop: $parse($attrs.onDrop),
            });

            dropContainer.addDropTarget(anchor, dropTarget);

            $scope.$on('$destroy', destroy);
        }
    };
})

.controller('DropTargetController', function () {
});
```

Yes, this directive is a little different. We add the `require` attribute to the DDO and assign it an array of directives whose functionality we want to include in the `drop-target` directive. The `^` at the beginning of `dropContainer` denotes the fact that we want to search the directive's parents for the controller. We also need to add `dropTarget` to the required dependencies. With this done, we then add a fourth parameter to the link function called `ctrls`. This parameter is an array that contains our two controllers, which we can access in the link function via `ctrls[0]` and `ctrls[1]`.

In the first two lines of the link function, we get our controllers from the `ctrls` parameter and assign them to local variables for use in our link function. Then we assign the `dropTarget` attribute to an `anchor` variable, and if the `dropTarget` attribute was left blank, we default `anchor` to `center`. Our last variable assignment takes the `removeDropTarget` method on the `dropContainer` controller and assigns it to the variable `destroy`. The second parameter that we passed to the `bind` method is an argument that will prepend any other arguments sent to the method that `bind` was called on. For example, if we called the `destroy` method as `destroy(x,y)`, the method would actually execute as if it had been called as `destroy(anchor, x, y)`.

This entire process is standard procedure for registering one directive with another directive; it's important that `drop-container` has access to `drop-target`, since the `updateDropTarget` method on the `drop-container` delegates events to `drop-target`.

Next, we add some classes that we'll use in the CSS to style our targets appropriately.

Then we call `init` on the `dropTarget` controller and pass in three parameters: the jQuery-wrapped DOM element on which the directive was defined, the link function's scope, and a list of callbacks that the controller can access and execute.

Two last bits and we're done with the link function. We call `addDropTarget` on the `DropContainerCtrl` and pass in the `anchor` variable (or basically the position of our dropTarget directive), and then pass in the drop-target instance. Lastly, we create an event listener that listens on $scope for the $destroy event, at which point our newly created destroy method will be invoked. Since we actually bound an argument to destroy when we defined it, calling destroy() will end up executing as destroy(anchor), which is what we want.

5.3.8   *Use the drop-target directive*

Now let's take a look at the HTML for the drop-target directive:

```
<!-- client/src/angello/storyboard/tmpl/storyboard.html -->
<li userstory
    ng-repeat="story in storyboard.stories | filter: {status:status.name}"
    drag-container="story" mime-type="application/x-angello-status"
    drop-container="" accepts="['application/x-angello-status']"
    class="story my-repeat-animation"
    ng-click="storyboard.setCurrentStory(story)">
<div drop-target="top"
    on-drag-enter="storyboard.insertAdjacent(story, data, true)"
    on-drop="storyboard.finalizeDrop(data)"></div>
<div drop-target="bottom"
    on-drag-enter="storyboard.insertAdjacent(story, data, false)"
    on-drop="storyboard.finalizeDrop(data)"></div>
    <!-- … -->
</li>
```

We define the drop-target directive and give it a position value like "top" or "bottom." Whenever a story is dragged over the "top" target on another story, it splices into the array above that story and vice versa. The splicing is controlled by the third parameter in the insertAdjacent method, which we'll examine shortly.

Then we add two more attributes, on-drag-enter and on-drop, and assign them callbacks that—you guessed it—get called when a drag-container is pulled over the drop-target area and when the drag-container is dropped in the drop-container area, respectively.

5.3.9   *Build the controller*

Let's move on to the controller, shall we?

```
// client/src/angello/storyboard/directives/DragAndDrop.js
angular.module('Angello.Storyboard')
    .controller('DropTargetController', function () {
        var dropTarget = this;

        dropTarget.init = function (el, scope, callbacks) {
            dropTarget.el = el;
            dropTarget.scope = scope;
            dropTarget.callbacks = callbacks;
        };
    });
```

As usual, we assign this to a dropTarget variable for usage in the rest of the controller.

The `init` method takes the passed-in element, scope, and callback functions and assigns them to the controller for further use:

```
// client/src/angello/storyboard/directives/DragAndDrop.js
angular.module('Angello.Storyboard')
    .controller('DropTargetController', function () {

        //...

        dropTarget.handleDragEnter = function (eventData) {
            dropTarget.el.addClass('drop-target-active');

            if (dropTarget.callbacks.onDragEnter) {
                dropTarget.callbacks
            ➥     .onDragEnter(dropTarget.scope, eventData);
            }
        };

        dropTarget.handleDragOver = function (eventData) {
            if (dropTarget.callbacks.onDragOver) {
                dropTarget.callbacks
            ➥     .onDragOver(dropTarget.scope, eventData);
            }
        };

        dropTarget.handleDragLeave = function (eventData) {
            dropTarget.el.removeClass('drop-target-active');

            if (dropTarget.callbacks.onDragLeave) {
                dropTarget.callbacks
            ➥     .onDragLeave(dropTarget.scope, eventData);
            }
        };

        dropTarget.handleDrop = function (eventData) {
            if (dropTarget.callbacks.onDrop) {
                dropTarget.callbacks.onDrop(dropTarget.scope, eventData);
            }
        };
    });
```

The rest of the methods in the controller follow the exact same convention: if the appropriate callback is available, execute it. The only deviation from this is in `handleDragEnter` and `handleDragLeave`, where we add/remove the `drop-target-active` class.

5.3.10 *Create the $dragging service*

The `$dragging` service is simply used to share data between the controllers of the `drag-container` and `drop-container` directives.

```
// client/src/angello/storyboard/directives/DragAndDrop.js
angular.module('Angello.Storyboard')
    .factory('$dragging', function () {
```

```
        var data = null;
        var type = null;

        return {
            getData: function () {
                return data;
            },
            getType: function () {
                return type;
            },
            setData: function (newData) {
                data = newData;
                return data;
            },
            setType: function (newType) {
                type = newType;
                return type;
            }
        };
    });
```

Here we define two variables, `data` and `type`, and expose them via a getter-setter API. The API has four methods: `getData`, `getType`, `setData`, and `setType`. As you would imagine, these methods return the `data` variable, return the `type` variable, set and return the `data` variable, and set and return the `type` variable. Pretty straightforward stuff.

5.3.11 *Update the StoryboardCtrl*

The last piece of the puzzle is the interaction between the `drop-container`/`drop-target` directives and the `StoryboardCtrl`. Both of the aforementioned directives have `on-drag-enter` and `on-drop` attributes that allow controller methods to be executed in those directives. Let's take a look at the methods passed to the `drop-target` directives: `insertAdjacent` and `finalizeDrop`:

```
// client/src/angello/storyboard/controllers/StoryboardController.js
angular.module('Angello.Storyboard')
    .controller('StoryboardCtrl',
        function ($scope, $log, StoriesModel, UsersModel,
                        STORY_STATUSES, STORY_TYPES) {

        //...

        storyboard.insertAdjacent = function (target, story, insertBefore) {
            if (target === story) return;

            var fromIdx = storyboard.stories.indexOf(story);
            var toIdx = storyboard.stories.indexOf(target);

            if (!insertBefore) toIdx++;

            if (fromIdx >= 0 && toIdx >= 0) {
                storyboard.stories.splice(fromIdx, 1);
```

```
                if (toIdx >= fromIdx) toIdx--;

                storyboard.stories.splice(toIdx, 0, story);

                story.status = target.status;
            }
        };

        storyboard.finalizeDrop = function (story) {
            StoriesModel.update(story.id, story)
                .then(function (result) {
                    $log.debug('RESULT', result);
                }, function (reason) {
                    $log.debug('REASON', reason);
                });
        };

        storyboard.changeStatus = function (story, status) {
            story.status = status.name;
        };

        //…
    });
```

Whenever a story is dragged over another story, the method assigned to the appropriate drop-target directive's on-drag-enter attribute is triggered (in our case, insert-Adjacent). This method takes three parameters—target, story, and insertBefore—and inserts a story properly in a status column (target and story actually come from the eventData object inside the dropContainer.updateDragTarget method). If the existing or target story is not the same as the story being moved, we then use their indices and the Boolean parameter insertBefore to place the story data at the proper position in the array for the status column.

The method assigned to the on-drop attribute of either a drop-container or drop-target directive is triggered when a story is dropped over that directive. This method just takes a story, grabs its ID, and updates the back end, notifying it of the status change.

A unique situation arises when the method assigned to the on-drag-enter attribute on the drop-container with class emptystatus is triggered. Since this directive has no stories in it, we don't have to figure out where in the array a story goes; we can simply change that story's status.

And that completes our foray into the drag-and-drop feature. We did a *lot* in this section, so let's do a quick review:

- We created three different directives: drag-container, drop-container, and drop-target.
- We defined a service called $dragging that lets you share data between the DragContainerController and the DropContainerController.
- You learned how to use JavaScript's .bind to execute a method in the context of a specific object.

- We used `$scope.$watch` and `$attrs.$observe` to listen for changes to attributes on our directives.
- We wrapped the code that changed AngularJS data in a `$scope.$apply` so that AngularJS knew to perform a digest cycle.
- We showed how to import a controller from another directive using `require` and how to use multiple controllers in the link function.
- You saw how `drop-container` and `drop-target` directives interacted with the `StoryboardCtrl`.

5.4   *Integrating with third-party libraries again!*

So far we've written two directives that relied on jQuery and jQuery UI, which has been a pleasant experience so far, but let's try for something more ambitious.

We'll build a directive that integrates with Flot and displays user story statistics—see figure 5.4.

> **FLOT**   Flot is a gorgeous graphing library that's built in JavaScript. You can read more about Flot at http://www.flotcharts.org/.

5.4.1   *Install Flot*

First we need to install Flot in our application. Flot comes with a core library, and then you add a plugin for the visualization you want to accomplish. In our case, we want to use the categories plugin because we want to segment our data based on categories.

We'll make Flot available to our application by adding references to the appropriate files in the following code:

```
// client/assets/js/boot.js
{ file: 'vendor/flot/jquery.flot.js' },
{ file: 'vendor/flot/jquery.flot.categories.js' },
```

The next two steps will go by pretty quickly, now that we've established muscle memory, but they're necessary steps to getting started.

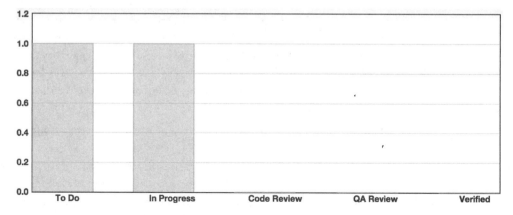

Figure 5.4   We may not have a lot, but we've got a Flot!

5.4.2 *Build the directive*

Call us creatures of habit, but we're going to start this directive the same way we kicked off the other two directives—with the basic skeleton:

```
// client/src/angello/dashboard/directives/ChartDirective.js
angular.module('Angello.Dashboard')
    .directive('chart',
        function () {
            var linker = function (scope, element, attrs) {
                // Link goes here
            };
            var controller = function($scope) {
                // Controller goes here
            };
            return {
                restrict: 'A',
                link: linker,
                controller: controller
            };
        });
```

5.4.3 *Use the directive*

We'll use the chart directive in two places, so we need to add it in two places:

```
<!-- client/src/angello/dashboard/tmpl/dashboard.html -->
<div class="container chart-wrapper">
    <h3>User Stories by Status</h3>
    <hr/>
    <div class="chart-container">
        <div chart class="chart-placeholder"></div>
    </div>
    <h3>User Stories by Type</h3>
    <hr/>
    <div class="chart-container">
        <div chart class="chart-placeholder"></div>
    </div>
</div>
```

5.4.4 *Massage our data*

Technically, the directive is working, but it doesn't actually do much yet. The interesting challenge with Flot integration is that Flot expects a very specific data structure to properly render the chart.

Here you can see the data structure that it expects, which was pulled from the Flot sample files:

```
var data = [
  ["January", 10],
  ["February", 8],
  ["March", 4],
  ["April", 13],
  ["May", 17],
  ["June", 9]
];
```

To make this work with the user stories, we need to come up with a data structure that looks like the following array:

```
var data = [
  ["Log", 1],
  ["To Do", 2],
  ["In Progress", 0],
  ["Code Review", 1],
  ["QA Review", 0],
  ["Verified", 1],
  ["Done", 1]
];
```

We'll delve into a pretty heavy utility function that will produce this very data structure. Bear with us and it'll make sense in a moment, and balance will be restored in the universe.

We'll unpack a heavy utility function that's used to produce the data structure that Flot needs. It's easiest to articulate what it does in natural language before we start to look at the code. In a nutshell, we tell parseDataForCharts to "Loop over Array A, and on each iteration, get the value that exists at Property A. Then, when you have that value, go to Array B and count how many times that value occurs on Property B, m'kay?"

```
// client/src/angello/dashboard/directives/ChartDirective.js
angular.module('Angello.Dashboard')
    .directive('chart',
        function () {
            var parseDataForCharts = function(sourceArray, sourceProp,
                referenceArray, referenceProp) {

                var data = [];
                referenceArray.each(function (r) {
                    var count = sourceArray.count(function (s) {
                        return s[sourceProp] == r[referenceProp];
                    });
                    data.push([r[referenceProp], count]);
                });
                return data;
            };
            //...
        });
```

The two main pieces of this function are the Sugar each method that iterates over the referenceArray and the Sugar count method that counts the matches between sourceArray[sourceProp] and referenceArray[referenceProp]. From there it's a matter of pushing the result in the right format into the data array for the return statement. Flot expects a format of [['property', number], ['property', number], etc], which we honor in the following line:

```
data.push([r[referenceProp], count]);
```

This was the part of the directive that got the most mind-share when it was being written, and now that we have our data in the format we need, it's going to be pretty much a matter of wiring up the pieces.

5.4.5 *It's time we had the "isolated scope talk"*

Scope, by default, prototypically inherits from its parent, and if we were to reference a property on the child scope, AngularJS would walk up the prototype chain until it found it. This is a non-issue in most cases, but there are times when you do want to isolate the directive's scope entirely from its parent scope to completely mitigate potential side effects.

AngularJS allows you to accomplish this via *isolated scope,* which creates an ironclad perimeter around the directive's scope, and then it's the responsibility of the developer to define exactly how the directive will communicate with the outside world. This essentially provides an API for your directive with clearly defined channels of communication.

There are three types of isolated scope: attribute-isolated scope, binding-isolated scope, and expression-isolated scope. *Attribute-isolated scope* binds on a single attribute, and communication is only from the parent to the child. The value that you define is interpreted as a string, and therefore is really only suitable for simple values. *Binding-isolated scope* enables two-way communication between the parent and child scope, and can bind to collections and objects as well as simple values. This is the most common type of isolated scope and is what most of the built-in AngularJS directives use. *Expression-isolated scope* works by allowing the child to execute an expression on the parent. Although not as common, expression-isolated scope is a great way to dynamically attach behavior to your application by letting the parent define the expression to be executed when the child calls the expression defined in the isolated scope.

> **GOING UP** We make an elevator pitch for isolated scope, and the topic warrants an entire discussion dedicated to it. Check out http://onehungrymind.com/ infographic-understanding-angularjs-isolated-scope for a more thorough examination of isolated scope and how it works.

Let's examine an instance of isolated scope as it relates to our project before we go any further:

```
// client/src/angello/dashboard/directives/ChartDirective.js
angular.module('Angello.Dashboard')
    .directive('chart',
        function () {
            //...
            return {
                restrict: 'A',
                link: linker,
                controller: controller,
                scope: {
                    sourceArray: '=',
                    referenceArray: '='
                }
            };
        });
```

We want to bind to `sourceArray` and `referenceArray` so that if they change, we'll know about it in the directive. Conversely, if we modified the arrays in the directive, we'd want the outside world to know as well. Isolated scope is accomplished on the definition object by passing in an object with the properties you want to expose and some special syntax to define the kind of isolation you want. In our case, we want binding-isolated scope and so we'll use an = sign to indicate this.

> **ISOLATED SCOPE**   Attribute-isolated scope is defined with an @ symbol, binding-isolated scope is defined with an equals sign (=), and expression-isolated scope is defined with an ampersand (&). If the property name you're isolating is the same to the outside world as what you're using internally, no other configuration is necessary. If for some reason you wanted to use a different name internally, then the format is as follows: externalProperty: '=internalProperty'.

We then exercise our right to isolated scope in the HTML:

```
<!-- client/src/angello/dashboard/tmpl/dashboard.html -->
<div class="container chart-wrapper">
    <h3>User Stories by Status</h3>
    <hr/>
    <div class="chart-container">
        <div chart class="chart-placeholder"
            source-array="dashboard.stories" source-prop="status"
            reference-array="dashboard.statuses" reference-prop="name">
        </div>
    </div>
    <h3>User Stories by Type</h3>
    <hr/>
    <div class="chart-container">
        <div chart class="chart-placeholder"
            source-array="dashboard.stories" source-prop="type"
            reference-array="dashboard.types" reference-prop="name">
        </div>
    </div>
</div>
```

We told the outside world to put any array in the source-array attribute, and the directive will internally treat it as sourceArray.

> **CAMEL CASE AND SNAKE CASE**   AngularJS converts JavaScript camel case into snake case in HTML. This is why in the directive we use sourceArray, and on the HTML it's source-array.

You may have noticed that we also define source-prop and reference-prop on the directive element, but we haven't set up isolated scope around these properties. This was a design decision that didn't warrant isolated scope, because those properties only need to be read once, and it's not worth incurring the cost of binding in any direction. We'll read them from the attrs array in the next section.

5.4.6   *Grand finale: breathe life into Flot*

And now that we've created communication channels with all of the data that we need, it's time to lock this down in style. It's time to actually hook up Flot:

```
// client/src/angello/dashboard/tmpl/dashboard.html
angular.module('Angello.Dashboard')
    .directive('chart', function () {
        //...
        var linker = function (scope, element, attrs) {
            scope.$watch('sourceArray', function () {
                scope.data = parseDataForCharts(
                    scope.sourceArray,
                    attrs['sourceProp'],
                    scope.referenceArray,
                    attrs['referenceProp']
                );

                if(element.is(':visible')){
                    $.plot(element, [ scope.data ], {
                        series: {
                            bars: {
                                show: true,
                                barWidth: 0.6,
                                align: "center"
                            }
                        },
                        xaxis: {
                            mode: "categories",
                            tickLength: 0
                        }
                    });
                }
            });
        };

        //...
});
```

The first thing we do is parse the data via our `parseDataForCharts` method, passing in our isolated scope arrays and the property values we read off of the `attrs` array. We set the result of that method call to the `data` property on `scope` so that we can use it when we spin up the Flot chart.

The one caveat about Flot is that the element it's drawing in has to be visible or it completely falls apart. That is why we use `element.is(':visible')` as a condition for proceeding any further. Then we instantiate Flot with `$.plot(element, [ scope.data ],` `{ });`, passing in `element`, `scope.data` and the appropriate configuration object.

BE INQUISITIVE When this directive was being created, we used the configuration object from the Flot sample files, and it works right out of the box. For fun, we encourage you to explore the different options that Flot has available, such as mouse interaction, colors, and so on.

Stop. Review time!

- We performed some more array wizardry with Sugar to get our data into a format that Flot could use.

- We talked about isolated scope and the benefits it provides.

- We instantiated Flot to show two completely different sets of data.

5.5   *Testing a directive*

The spec for a directive is actually a simple recipe: create an Angular element and then compile that element with $rootScope. We'll use our `userstory` directive as an example.

Let's begin by creating a `userStory` variable that will hold our directive's scope, an `element` variable that will contain our Angular element, a `StoriesModel` variable to reference the `StoriesModel` service, and lastly a `$rootScope` variable to, you guessed it, hold our root scope! Since the directive was declared on the `Angello.User` module, we also need to include that module:

```
client/tests/specs/directives/UserStoryDirective.spec.js
'use strict';

describe('userstory Directive', function () {
    var userStory,
        element,
        StoriesModel,
        $rootScope;

    beforeEach(module('Angello.User'));
});
```

Now we need to inject all of our dependencies. In a `beforeEach` call, we inject the $q, $compile, $rootScope, and StoriesModel references. We assign our global $root-Scope reference, create an Angular element out of HTML markup, and then compile the element with $rootScope.

Now remember how the controller-as syntax works? That's right, it creates a top-level object on $scope. So when a directive is defined using `controllerAs`, we can get its controller's methods and properties by calling the `scope` method on our compiled element and then getting the `userStory` property on that scope, since we defined our directive's `controllerAs` property as `userStory`.

We also spy on `StoriesModel.destroy`. Since we're not testing that service, we don't care what that method actually does, so we mock it out by calling `.and.call-Fake` and defining a simple function that returns a promise. In our directive, when `StoriesModel.destroy` is called successfully, we broadcast a `storyDeleted` event, so we spy on the `$broadcast` method on $rootScope:

```
client/tests/specs/directives/UserStoryDirective.spec.js
'use strict';

describe('userstory Directive', function () {

    //...

    beforeEach(inject(function($q, $compile, _$rootScope_, _StoriesModel_) {
```

```
    $rootScope = _$rootScope_;

    var directiveMarkup = angular.element('<li userstory></li>');
    element = $compile(directiveMarkup)($rootScope);
    userStory = element.scope().userStory;

    StoriesModel = _StoriesModel_;

    spyOn(StoriesModel, 'destroy').and.callFake(function() {
        var deferred = $q.defer();
        deferred.resolve('data');
        return deferred.promise;
    });

    spyOn($rootScope,'$broadcast').and.callThrough();
}));
});
```

As usual, the actual test is much more straightforward than the rigmarole needed to set it up. We simply call the deleteStory method on the directive's scope, pass it an argument with value 0, and then test to make sure that the method was indeed called with 0. We then resolve the promise using $rootScope.$digest() and then test to make sure the appropriate event was broadcasted:

```
client/tests/specs/directives/UserStoryDirective.spec.js
it('should delete a story', function() {
    userStory.deleteStory('0');
    expect(StoriesModel.destroy).toHaveBeenCalledWith('0');
    $rootScope.$digest();
    expect($rootScope.$broadcast).toHaveBeenCalledWith('storyDeleted');
});
```

> **Using bindToController**
>
> We've already talked about the controller-as syntax and why we use it. It turns out that there's a small disconnect between controllerAs in a directive DDO and isolate scope. If you use both of these features, you have to watch $scope for changes inside the controller and then update the this property whenever an attribute on isolate scope is changed. This completely defeats the purpose of controllerAs! In Angular 1.3, all you need to do is add bindToController: true to your DDO, and this will be updated every time an attribute on isolate scope is updated.

5.6 Best practices

DOM manipulation should be done in the link function and imperative logic in the controller. One of the advantages of using a JavaScript framework like AngularJS is the separation of concerns, especially the separation of the DOM from our imperative logic. We like to keep this theme rolling by putting all of the DOM manipulation logic in our directives' link function and all of our business logic in our directives' controller.

Favor a compartmentalized approach to writing directives. Oftentimes, we'll start building out a feature using a directive and then, perhaps a couple weeks later, we have a whale of a directive on our hands. It's not that our code is bad, it's just that our directive is doing too much at once. At this point, we like to break our directive into independent logical components and then use them together. This kills two birds with one stone: not only do we have cleaner, more maintainable code, but we can also reuse one or more of our components in other parts of the application.

5.7   *Summary*

And we have crossed the finish line with three directives we've built from the ground up. While we sacrificed covering the entire academic tome of directives in favor of illustrating practical, working examples, we hope that you've started to see the immense power of directives and dig deeper. Let's review:

- Directives allow you to extend HTML however you want.
- You learned what directives are, why you want them, and why you need them.
- There are three main parts to a directive: the *Directive Definition Object*, the *link function*, and the *controller*; you saw the purpose of each and how to use them.
- You learned what *isolated scope* is and how to leverage it in providing the maximum functionality to your directives.
- You saw how to include one directive's controller in the DDO of another directive and how to inject that controller into that directive's controller.
- You built complex features using directives, including a drag-and-drop feature and a third-party integration with a jQuery plugin to give you pretty graphs.

Animations

This chapter covers

- How AngularJS handles animations
- Understanding the animation-naming convention
- The three types of animations
- Concrete examples of each type as it relates to Angello

6.1 Intro to animations

AngularJS was originally created as a framework to handle enterprise CRUD applications. With the introduction of the new animations API, AngularJS has broadened the possibilities to offer something for designers and developers alike.

The most powerful aspect of AngularJS is directives, and AngularJS animations are essentially class-based directives that have the power to harness complex animations with the addition of a single class to your markup.

The goal of this chapter is to show you the AngularJS animation events, the naming convention around those events, and the three types of animations you can do in AngularJS, with practical examples for each. We're not going to examine CSS3 animations or JavaScript animations in depth, but rather endeavor to lay a strong foundation that you can let your creativity run wild on.

6.1.1 How AngularJS handles animations

AngularJS animations can be distilled down to five events and a class-based naming convention. Once you've grasped the events at play and the naming convention, AngularJS animations fade into the background and the animations themselves take center stage.

There are three types of animations that you can create with AngularJS: CSS transitions, CSS animations, and JavaScript animations. Each type of animation is well suited for varying contexts, and we'll explore each of them later in the chapter.

AngularJS doesn't actually do any of the animations themselves, but simply provides the hooks for you to apply your own animations as you see fit. These hooks come in the form of *events*, and there are only five of them.

The five animation events are `enter`, `leave`, `move`, `addClass`, and `removeClass` (see table 6.1).

Table 6.1 The AngularJS animation furious five

Event	Function	Description
enter	`$animate.enter(element, parent, after, callback);`	Appends the `element` object after the `after` node or within the parent node and then runs the `enter` animation on the element
leave	`$animate.leave(element, callback);`	Runs the `leave` animation and then removes the element from the DOM
move	`$animate.move(element, parent, after, callback);`	Moves the `element` node either after the `after` node or inside of the `v` node and then runs the `move` animation on the element
addClass	`$animate.addClass(element, className, callback);`	Runs the `addClass` animation based on the `className` value and then adds the class to the element
removeClass	`$animate.removeClass(element, className, callback);`	Runs the `removeClass` animation based on the `className` value and then removes the class from the element

The `enter` and `leave` events are fired when a DOM element is added or removed from the DOM tree, respectively. The `move` event is fired when a DOM element changes position within the DOM tree. Last but not least, the `addClass` and `removeClass` events are fired when a class is added to or removed from an element, respectively.

6.1.2 The animation-naming convention

AngularJS animations are entirely class-based, which is a design decision that makes integration with third-party libraries easier. Even JavaScript animations follow a class-based naming convention for consistency.

The animation-naming convention follows a [class]-[event]-[state] pattern, as shown in figure 6.1. This figure indicates that we're dealing with a mute class that's being added and removed, as seen by `.mute-add` and `.mute-remove`. The animation defaults to the starting state and then progresses to the active state, as in "the class has been actively applied." The starting state is `.mute-add`, and `.mute-add-active` is the active or completed state.

.[class]-[event]-[state]

.mute-add

.mute-add-active

.mute-remove

.mute-remove-active

Figure 6.1 The animation-naming convention applied to directives

If your animations are defined within CSS and the events are triggered by an AngularJS directive such as `ng-if` or `ng-repeat`, then the class name will be prefixed with an *ng*, as in `ng-enter` and `ng-leave`.

6.1.3 Animations enable!

The most logical place to start from a pragmatic sense is with how you enable animations within your AngularJS application. AngularJS animations aren't part of the AngularJS core, and so you have to include that as a separate file. We'll use GreenSock Animation Platform (GSAP), which is a JavaScript animation framework. We want the TweenMax library, which contains everything GreenSock has to offer.

```
// client/assets/js/boot.js
{ file:
    '//cdnjs.cloudflare.com/ajax/libs/
    ➥   angular.js/1.3.3/angular-animate.min.js'
},
{ file:
    '//cdnjs.cloudflare.com/ajax/libs/gsap/latest/TweenMax.min.js'
},
```

> **GREENSOCK** You can read more about GreenSock at http://www.greensock.com/gsap-js/.

Now that angular-animate.min.js has been included, we need to inject it as a sub-module into our application:

```
// client/src/angello/Angello.js
var myModule = angular.module('Angello', [
    //...
    'ngAnimate',
    //...
]);
```

With those two steps completed, we're ready to start adding animations to our application.

6.2   *CSS transitions*

The easiest animations to implement are CSS transitions. The ease of implementation comes from the fact that they're entirely CSS-based and much more concise to express than CSS animations.

We'll create a my-fade animation and apply it to a div that will trigger the animation when the div is added or removed from the DOM via ng-if. This animation will toggle the visibility of the story details in the right column when the Angello application is running in storyboard mode (see table 6.2).

Table 6.2   The animation-naming convention

Event	Starting CSS class	Ending CSS class	Directives that fire it
enter	.ng-enter	.ng-enter-active	ngRepeat, ngInclude, ngIf, ngView
leave	.ng-leave	.ng-leave-active	ngRepeat, ngInclude, ngIf, ngView
move	.ng-move	.ng-move-active	ngRepeat

6.2.1   *Define the base transition*

The first thing you need to do when constructing a CSS transition within AngularJS is set up the base transition. Because we're using ng-if to trigger the animation and the event is caused by an AngularJS directive, we need to define the classes for ng-enter and ng-leave:

```
/* client/assets/css/animations.css */
.my-fade-animation.ng-enter, .my-fade-animation.ng-leave {
    -webkit-transition: 0.5s linear all;
    -moz-transition: 0.5s linear all;
    -o-transition: 0.5s linear all;
    transition: 0.5s linear all;
}
```

In this code we define the transition for ng-enter and ng-leave on the my-fade animation to use linear easing that lasts for 0.5 seconds and applies to all properties.

6.2.2   *Define the ng-enter transitions*

The next step is to define the starting and stopping states for ng-enter. We'll start with an opacity of 0 and finish with an opacity of 1. This means that when the element is added, it'll start completely transparent and then fade in to full opacity.

```
/* client/assets/css/animations.css */
.my-fade-animation.ng-enter {
    opacity: 0;
}

.my-fade-animation.ng-enter.ng-enter-active {
    opacity: 1;
}
```

6.2.3 *Define the ng-leave transitions*

We'll now define the transition for `ng-leave`, which is usually the reverse of what you did for `ng-enter`. We'll start with an opacity of 1 and end with an opacity of 0:

```
.my-fade-animation.ng-leave {
    opacity: 1;
}

.my-fade-animation.ng-leave.ng-leave-active {
    opacity: 0;
}
```

For the sake of illustration, we've separated the `ng-enter` and `ng-leave` classes, but you could easily combine them for conciseness:

```
.my-fade-animation.ng-enter,
.my-fade-animation.ng-leave.ng-leave-active {
    opacity: 0;
}

.my-fade-animation.ng-leave,
.my-fade-animation.ng-enter.ng-enter-active {
    opacity: 1;
}
```

6.2.4 *Making it move*

Now that the CSS classes have been defined, it's a matter of attaching them to the DOM for use. Now you'll see what we mean when we say AngularJS transitions are essentially class-based directives that encapsulate animation functionality.

This is the HTML without the animation:

```
<!-- client/src/angello/storyboard/tmpl/storyboard.html -->
<div class="details">
    <!-- ... -->

    <div ng-if="storyboard.detailsVisible">
        <!-- ... -->
    </div>
</div>
```

This is the HTML with the animation:

```
<!-- client/src/angello/storyboard/tmpl/storyboard.html -->
<div class="details">
    <!-- ... -->

    <div ng-if="storyboard.detailsVisible" class="my-fade-animation">
        <!-- ... -->
    </div>
</div>
```

And so the only part left in this section is to actually toggle ng-if:

```
// client/src/angello/storyboard/controllers/StoryboardController.js
angular.module('Angello.Storyboard')
    .controller('StoryboardCtrl',
        function ($scope, $log, StoriesModel, UsersModel,
                  STORY_STATUSES, STORY_TYPES) {
        //...
        storyboard.detailsVisible = true;
        //...
        storyboard.setDetailsVisible = function (visible) {
            storyboard.detailsVisible = visible;
        };
});
```

In the StoryboardCtrl, we create a property on our $scope reference, called detailsVisible, that we'll use to bind ng-if to. We also create a method called set-DetailsVisible that we use to set detailsVisible to true or false based on the value of the visible parameter.

In the HTML, we bind to detailsVisible via ng-if="storyboard.detailsVisible":

```
<!-- client/src/angello/storyboard/tmpl/storyboard.html -->
<div class="details">
    <div class="details-nav">
        <div ng-if="!storyboard.detailsVisible">
            <button class="btn pull-left btn-default"
                    ng-click="storyboard.setDetailsVisible(true)">
                <span class="glyphicon glyphicon-arrow-left"></span>
            </button>
        </div>
        <div ng-if="storyboard.detailsVisible">
            <button class="btn pull-right btn-default"
                    ng-click="storyboard.setDetailsVisible(false)">
                <span class="glyphicon glyphicon-arrow-right"></span>
            </button>
        </div>
    </div>

    <div ng-if="storyboard.detailsVisible"
 class="my-fade-animation">
        <!-- ... -->
    </div>
</div>
```

Note that we also have two other divs that are being toggled based on the property of detailsVisible. If detailsVisible is true, then the button to set detailsVisible to false is shown, and vice versa.

We've now completed the functionality for attaching a CSS transition to our application. In the next section we'll cover another animation, but this time we'll do it with a CSS animation.

6.3   *CSS animations*

Now that you've seen AngularJS animations using CSS transitions, let's build on that
with another animation using CSS animations. CSS animations tend to be more verbose than CSS transitions, but they're also significantly more powerful.

For this example, we'll do another fade animation, but this time with `ng-repeat`. If
you recall, in table 6.2 `ng-repeat` has three events that we need to style for. These
three events are `ng-enter`, `ng-leave`, and `ng-move`.

6.3.1   *Define the base animation classes*

The first thing we need to do is to define the base animation classes:

```
/* client/assets/css/animations.css */
.my-repeat-animation.ng-enter {
  -webkit-animation: 0.5s repeat-animation-enter;
  -moz-animation: 0.5s repeat-animation-enter;
  -o-animation: 0.5s repeat-animation-enter;
  animation: 0.5s repeat-animation-enter;
}

.my-repeat-animation.ng-leave {
  -webkit-animation: 0.5s repeat-animation-leave;
  -moz-animation: 0.5s repeat-animation-leave;
  -o-animation: 0.5s repeat-animation-leave;
  animation: 0.5s repeat-animation-leave;
}

.my-repeat-animation.ng-move {
  -webkit-animation: 0.5s repeat-animation-move;
  -moz-animation: 0.5s repeat-animation-move;
  -o-animation: 0.5s repeat-animation-move;
  animation: 0.5s repeat-animation-move;
}
```

We define our base CSS class as `my-repeat-animation` and then define animations
for `ng-enter`, `ng-leave`, and `ng-move`. We then define the animation property with
a 0.5-second duration and the appropriate keyframe for the animation.

> **VENDOR PREFIXES**   The reason why CSS animations are so verbose is because
> you have to define the animation for every vendor prefix. Using a CSS prepro-
> cessor such as Sass or Less eliminates the need to type all of this out by hand.

6.3.2   *Define the animation keyframes*

Now that the base animation classes are defined, it's just a matter of defining the key-
frames with the from and to states defined. Also, with CSS animations, it's not necessary to use the active convention that CSS transitions use.

The following is a fairly lengthy piece of code, but the pattern is easy to identify.
The `ng-enter` animations go from 0 opacity to an opacity of 1, while `ng-leave` does
the exact opposite, and `ng-move` goes from an opacity of 0.5 to an opacity of 1:

```css
/* client/assets/css/animations.css */
@keyframes repeat-animation-enter {
  from {
    opacity:0;
  }
  to {
    opacity:1;
  }
}

@-webkit-keyframes repeat-animation-enter {
  from {
    opacity:0;
  }
  to {
    opacity:1;
  }
}

@-moz-keyframes repeat-animation-enter {
  from {
    opacity:0;
  }
  to {
    opacity:1;
  }
}

@-o-keyframes repeat-animation-enter {
  from {
    opacity:0;
  }
  to {
    opacity:1;
  }
}

@keyframes repeat-animation-leave {
  from {
    opacity:1;
  }
  to {
    opacity:0;
  }
}

@-webkit-keyframes repeat-animation-leave {
  from {
    opacity:1;
  }
  to {
    opacity:0;
  }
}
```

```
@-moz-keyframes repeat-animation-leave {
  from {
    opacity:1;
  }
  to {
    opacity:0;
  }
}

@-o-keyframes repeat-animation-leave {
  from {
    opacity:1;
  }
  to {
    opacity:0;
  }
}

@keyframes repeat-animation-move {
  from {
    opacity:0.5;
  }
  to {
    opacity:1;
  }
}

@-webkit-keyframes repeat-animation-move {
  from {
    opacity:0.5;
  }
  to {
    opacity:1;
  }
}

@-moz-keyframes repeat-animation-move {
  from {
    opacity:0.5;
  }
  to {
    opacity:1;
  }
}

@-o-keyframes repeat-animation-move {
  from {
    opacity:0.5;
  }
  to {
    opacity:1;
  }
}
```

6.3.3   *Make it move*

To show the portability of AngularJS animations, we can actually attach the same animation to two different `ng-repeat` instances with little fanfare:

```html
<!-- client/src/angello/storyboard/tmpl/storyboard.html -->
<div class="list-area-animation"
     ng-class="{'list-area-expanded':!storyboard.detailsVisible}">
    <div class="list-wrapper">
        <ul class="list my-repeat-animation"
            ng-repeat="status in storyboard.statuses">
            <h3 class="status">{{status.name}}</h3>
            <hr/>
            <li userstory
                ng-repeat="story in storyboard.stories
               ➥    | filter:{status:status.name}"
                drag-container="story"
               ➥    mime-type="application/x-angello-status"
                drop-container=""
               ➥    accepts="['application/x-angello-status']"
                class="story my-repeat-animation"
                ng-click="storyboard.setCurrentStory(story)">

                <!-- ... -->
            </li>
        </ul>
    </div>
</div>
```

We attach it to the `ul` items, which render the status columns that the user stories are organized into, and to the `li` items that represent the user stories themselves.

We asserted at the beginning of the chapter that AngularJS animations are just a matter of a handful of events and a naming convention. We believe that this section really proved it in the sense that we haven't introduced any new concepts other than the CSS animation syntax itself. It was to a point anticlimactic, because by now some of these elements should start to feel familiar.

6.4   *JavaScript animations*

The final type in the AngularJS animations triad is JavaScript animations. For this example we'll toggle the position of the details section by animating it on and off the screen. We'll accomplish this by dynamically attaching a `details-visible` class using `ng-class`.

You can see the details section shown in figure 6.2, and in figure 6.3 it's in its hidden state.

You can use any JavaScript animation library, but for our example we'll use Tween-Max, which is a part of the GreenSock Animation Platform. TweenMax is an incredibly powerful and feature-rich animation library that performs well on desktop and mobile browsers.

Figure 6.2   Details shown

Figure 6.3   Details hidden

6.4.1   *Defining the JavaScript animation*

JavaScript animations are defined using the `animation` service:

```
// client/src/angello/app/animations/DetailsAnimation.js
angular.module('Angello.Common')
    .animation('.details-animation',
        function () {
            //...
        });
```

Defining the animation is similar to defining an AngularJS service or controller.
The only difference is that the animation name is class-based, so instead of `details-
animation`, it's `.details-animation`.

6.4.2 *The JavaScript animation events*

Now that the animation has been defined, we need to actually configure it to handle the animation events. Because we trigger the animation with ng-class, the two events we want to listen to are addClass and removeClass:

```
// client/src/angello/app/animations/DetailsAnimation.js
angular.module('Angello.Common')
    .animation('.details-animation',
        function () {
            return {
                addClass: function (element, className, done) {
                    //...
                },
                removeClass: function (element, className, done) {
                    //...
                }
            };
        });
```

The event handlers are defined inline to the return object. The three parameters that each handler receives are element, className, and done. The element is the DOM element that the event was triggered on, className is the name of the class that triggered the event, and done is the callback function that needs to be called when the animation is complete.

6.4.3 *The JavaScript animation class*

It's possible to have more than one animation defined on an element, and so it's necessary to perform some logic to only act if the class that triggered the event is the one you've defined:

```
// client/src/angello/app/animations/DetailsAnimation.js
angular.module('Angello.Common')
    .animation('.details-animation',
        function () {
            return {
                addClass: function (element, className, done) {
                    if (className == 'details-visible') {
                        //...
                    }
                    else {
                        done();
                    }
                },
                removeClass: function (element, className, done) {
                    if (className == 'details-visible') {
                        //...
                    }
                    else {
                        done();
                    }
                }
            };
        });
```

This is why, in the preceding code, we check to see if className is equal to details-visible, and if it's not then we call the done callback.

6.4.4 TweenMax

Now that we know that we're dealing with the details-visible class specifically, it's time to add in the TweenMax code to actually do the animation work:

```
// client/src/angello/app/animations/DetailsAnimation.js
angular.module('Angello.Common')
    .animation('.details-animation',
        function () {
            return {
                addClass: function (element, className, done) {
                    if (className == 'details-visible') {
                        TweenMax.to(element, 0.5,
                            {right: 0, onComplete: done });
                    } else {
                        done();
                    }
                },
                removeClass: function (element, className, done) {
                    if (className == 'details-visible') {
                        TweenMax.to(element, 0.5, {
                            right: -element.width() + 50,
                            onComplete: done
                        });
                    } else {
                        done();
                    }
                }
            };
        });
```

When details-visible is added, we use TweenMax to animate the element to an absolute position of 0 pixels to the right. When details-visible is removed, we use TweenMax to animate it off the screen by setting the right property to the negative value of element.width() plus 50 pixels so the Show button is still visible.

6.4.5 Making it move

The final piece to make the details-animation work is to add it to the DOM and set ng-class to toggle the details-visible class.

The following is the same code we used earlier, but with a few small additions to the outer div. We've added details-animation to the class attribute, so now the animation has a hook into the DOM. And we're also dynamically adding or removing the details-visible class based on the value of detailsVisible with ng-class="{'details-visible':storyboard.detailsVisible}":

```
<!-- client/src/angello/storyboard/tmpl/storyboard.html -->
<div class="details details-animation"
    ng-class="{'details-visible':storyboard.detailsVisible}">
```

```
<div class="details-nav">
    <div ng-if="!storyboard.detailsVisible">
        <button class="btn pull-left btn-default"
                ng-click="storyboard.setDetailsVisible(true)">
            <span class="glyphicon glyphicon-arrow-left"></span>
        </button>
    </div>
    <div ng-if="storyboard.detailsVisible">
        <button class="btn pull-right btn-default"
                ng-click="storyboard.setDetailsVisible(false)">
            <span class="glyphicon glyphicon-arrow-right"></span>
        </button>
    </div>
</div>

<div ng-if="storyboard.detailsVisible" class="my-fade-animation">
<!-- ... -->
</div>
</div>
```

The resulting animation works in conjunction with the CSS transition animation we defined so that the details elements fade out as the details section slides off the screen, and fade in as the details section slides back in.

MANUALLY TRIGGERED ANIMATIONS   You can manually trigger your own animations using the $animate service. See http://docs.angularjs.org/api/ngAnimate .$animate for more details.

6.5   *Testing*

Because animations target the visual aspect of our application more than the functionality aspect, we usually leave animations out of our unit tests. But if you'd like to know how to test animations, visit http://www.yearofmoo.com/2013/08/remastered-animation-in-angularjs-1-2.html#testing-animations.

Full-page animations

Here's a super easy way to get full-page transitions: set an animation class on the tag with the `ng-view` directive defined on it. In the context of Angello, if you were to find the `<div ng-view=""></div>` element in `index.html` and add `class="my-fade-animation"`, each route would automatically start fading in and out!

6.6   *Best practices*

Memorize the naming conventions for AngularJS animations. Seriously, you'll be an animation alchemist. You'll be able to throw together pro animations in no time at all.

   Use CSS transitions/animations when possible. We like to use CSS transitions and animations for simpler visuals, and only build them using JavaScript when they involve multiple animations and/or complex transitions. That way, we can keep our styles in our CSS files and let the JavaScript focus on the business logic.

6.7 *Summary*

Now that you have three examples under your belt, we hope that it's easy to identify the event and naming-convention patterns that surround AngularJS animations. AngularJS has proven itself time and time again to be a great framework for doing functional things, but animations bring some fashion to that functionality with an easy-to-use API that leverages all CSS and JavaScript to do any kind of animation you can imagine. Let's do a quick recap:

- There are five animation event hooks in AngularJS: `enter`, `leave`, `move`, `addClass`, and `removeClass`.
- You learned what triggers each type of event.
- You discovered the naming conventions that make animations tick.
- You viewed examples of CSS transitions, CSS animations, and animations using JavaScript.
- You got a quick introduction to TweenMax and how it interacts with AngularJS.

7

Structuring your site with routes

This chapter covers

- Components of AngularJS routes
- Creating routes
- Route parameters
- Creating and resolving dependencies in routes
- Route events

Angello is starting to grow in complexity, with distinct but related areas of functionality such as managing users, managing user stories, and displaying visualizations. How do you know when to show the user and when to show the user stories? What if you want to show just the user stories for a specific user? This can get complex as you try to account for all the possible permutations.

Every web application has a URL, and you can use this to define the state of the application. Based on the URL, you can intelligently route the user to the part of the application that they want to see. This technique is called *URL routing*, and AngularJS allows you to implement routing in your web applications with the ngRoute sub-module. Routes help you intelligently decide what to show and how to show it, based on the URL of the application. We'll spend the rest of this chapter discussing the various parts that make routes possible in AngularJS, while showing how we can use it in Angello.

7.1   *The components of AngularJS routes*

Routing in AngularJS consists of four components that work together to allow you to use URL routes to control the state of your application. See figure 7.1 and table 7.1 for the big picture of how these components work together.

Table 7.1 `ngRoute` **components**

Component	Responsibility
`$routeProvider`	Configures routes
`$route`	Listens to URL changes and coordinates with the `ng-view` instance
`ng-view`	Responsible for coordinating the creation of the appropriate controller and view for the current route
`$routeParams`	Interprets and communicates URL parameters to the controller

You'll see all of these components in action in a moment, but a high-level example would be if, say, you wanted to see the user stories assigned to a specific user. You'd use `$routeProvider` to configure a route with the `$route` service to detect when the URL is pointing to a specific user such as `/users/123`, with `123` being the user's ID. `$route` will detect this route and work with `ng-view` to create the appropriate controller and view to display the user's stories. The `$routeParams` service is injected into the controller and exposes the user's ID from the URL so that the controller can act upon it.

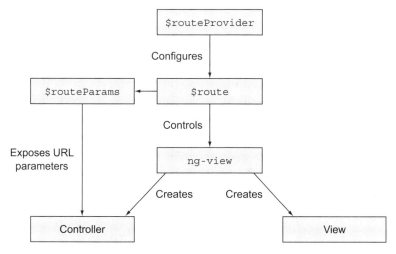

Figure 7.1 `ngRoute` **big picture**

7.2 *How to create routes in AngularJS*

Now that we've identified the major components of ngRoute, it's time to set up a few routes within our Angello application so we can navigate from page to page. We'll start out with a basic implementation and build from that foundation.

7.2.1 *Create your first route with ngRoute and ngView*

Because ngRoute isn't part of the AngularJS core, the first thing we need to do is to include the ngRoute source file. You can download the source file directly from the AngularJS website or use the CDN or Bower to fetch the file:

```
// client/assets/js/boot.js
{ file:
    '//cdnjs.cloudflare.com/ajax/libs/angular.js/1.3.3/angular-route.min.js'
},
```

Now that we've included the source file, we need to reference the sub-module in our application module definition:

```
// client/src/angello/Angello.js
var myModule = angular.module('Angello',
    [
        'ngRoute',
        //...
    ]);
```

7.2.2 *Add ngView*

One final piece before we start defining our routes: we need to tell Angello where we want to display the route's rendered template in our application:

```
 <!-- client/index.html -->
<body ng-controller="MainCtrl as main" ng-class="{loading:loadingView}">
    <!-- ... -->
    <div ng-view=""></div>
    <!-- ... -->
</body>
```

We accomplish this by adding <div ng-view=""></div> into our main layout file. ngView is responsible for fetching the route template and compiling it with the route's controller and displaying the finished, compiled view to the user.

> **COMPLEX LAYOUTS**   The relationship between a route and a view is one-to-one, which can be a significant disadvantage if you have a complex layout that requires nested views. A great solution to this problem is to use AngularUI Router: https://github.com/angular-ui/ui-router.

7.2.3 *Set up your route with $routeProvider*

The first route that we need to set up is for the root of Angello, since this is the entry point for the entire application. The path for this route will follow standard web conventions and consist of a single forward slash. We'll define the template we want to use for the view and the controller that we need to control that view.

PLANNING YOUR ROUTES   Routes are always configured in the config block of the module, because it's behavior that needs to be available as soon as the application runs.

Routes are primarily configured using the when method provided by $routeProvider. The when method takes two arguments: the path parameter and the route configuration object. The path parameter defines the URL pattern that the route will match against, and the route configuration object defines how the matched route is supposed to be handled.

We call
$routeProvider.when()
to set up a new route
with a path parameter
of / to indicate the
root of our web
application.

We set up our routes
in the config block of
the module, so this is
where we begin.

```
// client/src/angello/Angello.js
myModule.config(
    function ($routeProvider, $httpProvider, $provide) {
      $routeProvider
        .when('/', {
            templateUrl: 'src/angello/storyboard/
              tmpl/storyboard.html',
            controller: 'StoryboardCtrl',
            controllerAs: 'storyboard'
        });
});
```

We need to define a
template for our
route, so in our route
configuration object
we set the
templateUrl property
with a value of views/
storyboard.html.

The second part we define on the
route configuration object is the
controller for the view, so we set
controller to StoryboardCtrl and
define how we want the controller
to be referenced in the view
(storyboard in this case).

Now that we've set up the base route for Angello, we need to set up a way for the viewer to get to the dashboard and users view. We can apply the same templateUrl and controller pattern to accomplish this. The following code illustrates this in action:

```
// client/src/angello/Angello.js
myModule.config(function ($routeProvider, $httpProvider, $provide) {
    $routeProvider
        .when('/', {
            templateUrl: 'src/angello/storyboard/tmpl/storyboard.html',
            controller: 'StoryboardCtrl',
            controllerAs: 'storyboard'
        })
        .when('/dashboard', {
            templateUrl: 'src/angello/dashboard/tmpl/dashboard.html',
            controller: 'DashboardCtrl',
            controllerAs: 'dashboard'
        })
        .when('/users', {
            templateUrl: 'src/angello/user/tmpl/users.html',
```

```
        controller: 'UsersCtrl',
        controllerAs: 'users'
    })
    .otherwise({redirectTo: '/'});    ◄─┐     ❶
});
```

What happens if a user tries to go to a route that doesn't exist? $routeProvider comes with an additional method called otherwise that's used when a route doesn't match any other definition. In the preceding code ❶, we call redirectTo from within other-wise to navigate back to the root of the application if no matching route is found.

7.2.4   *Set up route navigation*

Now that we have our routes defined, it's time to modify our navigation so that we can navigate to the routes in our application. By default, AngularJS uses a hash symbol such as #/users as a reference point for a route. To navigate to the root of the site, we therefore would use <a href="#/"></a> to accomplish the task.

```
<!-- client/index.html -->
<div class="navbar navbar-fixed-top navbar-default">
    <div class="navbar-header">
        <a class="logo navbar-brand" href="#/">
            <img src="assets/img/angello.png">
        </a>
    </div>
    <div class="btn-group pull-right" ng-show="main.currentUser">
        <a class="btn btn-danger" href="#/">
            <span class="glyphicon glyphicon-home"></span>
        </a>
        <a class="btn btn-danger" href="#/users">
            <span class="glyphicon glyphicon-user"></span>
        </a>
        <a class="btn btn-danger" href="#/dashboard">
            <span class="glyphicon glyphicon-signal"></span>
        </a>
        <button class="btn btn-default" ng-click="main.logout()">
            <span class="glyphicon glyphicon-log-out"></span>
        </button>
    </div>
</div>
```

Favor anchor tags over programmatically setting routes using $location. Program-matically setting routes breaks a lot of accepted UX patterns such as opening a new tab upon link click.

7.2.5   *Review*

We've just set up three routes for Angello so we can navigate to the storyboard view, the dashboard view, and the users view. To do this, we added ngRoute to our appli-cation, set up ngView, and defined our routes with $routeProvider. We added ngRoute to Angello so that the entire application could have routing functionality. We added ngView to the main HTML page so that ngRoute would know where to

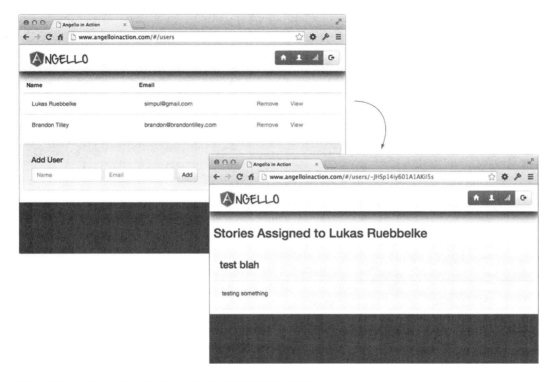

Figure 7.2 Using route parameters to get detailed information

render the templates for each route. We then defined our routes in the `module.con-fig` block using `$routeProvider`. And finally, we updated our navigation to point to the appropriate routes.

7.3 Using parameters with routes

We're using routes to define the state of the application, and often we need to use routes to define dynamic portions of the application state. In Angello, we have a view that we want to use to show the user stories assigned to the user, so we need to know what user we need to render the view for (see figure 7.2).

A route path can contain named groups that are delineated with a colon; for example, `:userId`. `$route` will attempt to match the path against `$location.path` and any matched parameters will be stored in the `$routeParams` service to be injected into the appropriate controller. See figure 7.3.

If the current URL is `/users/123`, then `$routeParams` will have a `userId` property with a value of `123`.

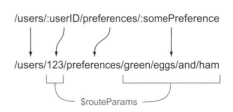

Figure 7.3 The anatomy of route parameters

And so let's add this exact capability to Angello by creating a route for a single user:

```
// client/src/angello/Angello.js
myModule.config(function ($routeProvider, $httpProvider, $provide) {
    $routeProvider
        //...
        .when('/users/:userId', {
            templateUrl: 'src/angello/user/tmpl/user.html',
            controller: 'UserCtrl',
            controllerAs: 'myUser'
        })
        //...
        .otherwise({redirectTo: '/'});
});
```

We'll set the path to /users/:userId, which will attach a userId property to $routeParams so we can use it in the UserCtrl.

Now that we've defined the variable in our user route, we need to evaluate it so it's available as a $scope variable in our UserCtrl:

```
// client/src/angello/user/controllers/UserController.js
angular.module('Angello.User')
    .controller('UserCtrl',
        function ('$routeParams') {
            var myUser = this;

            myUser.userId = $routeParams['userId'];
        });
```

To read route parameters, we need to inject the $routeParams service in our controller. The property userId exists on $routeParams, and we can assign the value to myUser.userId by evaluating $routeParams['userId'].

We've been approaching route parameters from the inside out, but how do you actually set a parameter on a route? How do you set userId so that you can use it in the users view? The solution is simply a matter of properly crafting a URL link, and AngularJS makes this even easier!

```
<!-- client/src/angello/user/tmpl/users.html -->
<tr ng-repeat="user in users.users">
    <!-- ... -->
    <td>
        <button type="button" class="btn btn-link"
                ng-click="users.removeUser(user.id)">Remove</button>
        <a class="btn btn-link" href="#/users/{{user.id}}">View</a>
    </td>
</tr>
```

The entry point to the user view will be the users view, and in that page we know about all our users and their IDs. From within our ng-repeat, we'll add a new link that points to #/users/, and because we have access to the user's ID, we can bind to it via {{user.id}} to make a complete link of href="#/users/{{user.id}}".

7.3.1 Review

You've just learned how to use the application's URL as a mechanism for evaluating and passing values from one view to another. We used this technique in Angello to pass a userId variable from the users view to the user view so that we could get specific information for that user. We also saw data binding in action in our users view to dynamically construct the links to the user view with the appropriate userId value for each user.

7.4 Using resolve with routes

One challenge with Angello is that we want to load a user's available information and a collection of stories to work with before we show the user view. AngularJS allows us to handle this situation by defining dependencies on our routes that must be resolved before the route's controller is instantiated.

At a high level, we want to make sure that the user view is given the correct user from the users view, as well as provide all available stories so that we can assign the correct stories to the provided user. We'll use the resolve property on the route configuration object (the object that's passed as the second argument to $routeProvider.when) to define this dependency. The resolve property is an object map that allows us to define multiple dependencies.

```
// client/src/angello/Angello.js
myModule.config(function ($routeProvider, $httpProvider, $provide) {
    $routeProvider
        //...
        .when('/users/:userId', {
            templateUrl: 'src/angello/user/tmpl/user.html',
            controller: 'UserCtrl',
            controllerAs: 'myUser',
            resolve: {
                user: function ($route, $routeParams, UsersModel) {
                    var userId = $route.current.params['userId']
                                 ? $route.current.params['userId']
                                 : $routeParams['userId'];
                    return UsersModel.fetch(userId);
                },
                stories: function (StoriesModel) {
                    return StoriesModel.all();
                }
            }
        })
        //...
        .otherwise({redirectTo: '/'});
});
```

We declare a user property and inject $route, $routeParams, and UsersModel.

We declare a stories property and inject StoriesModel.

We're able to extract the userId using $route or $routeParams just like we would in a controller.

We call UsersModel.fetch to get the user for userId.

The stories property will be resolved with the values of the StoriesService.find call.

The interesting piece about this code is that because UsersModel.fetch(userId) and StoriesModel.all() are returning a promise, we can attach a then method to be called when the promise resolves. At this point we'll be able to interact with both of these values in the controller. Boom!

And now let's jump over to the `UserCtrl` to see the user and stories dependencies being used:

```
// client/src/angello/user/controllers/UserController.js
angular.module('Angello.User')
    .controller('UserCtrl',
        function ($routeParams, user, stories) {
            //...
            myUser.user = user.data;

            myUser.getAssignedStories = function (userId, stories) {
                var assignedStories = {};

                Object.keys(stories, function(key, value) {
                    if (value.assignee == userId) {
                        assignedStories[key] = stories[key];
                    }
                });

                return assignedStories;
            };

            myUser.stories =
            ➥ myUser.getAssignedStories(myUser.userId, stories);
        });
```

Dependencies defined in the route configuration object are injected just like other services. From within the controller, we can now use these properties at our discretion. In the preceding code, we simply bind the requested user's data to `myUser.user` for use in the view; then we take that same data and, in conjunction with the injected stories collection, get all of the stories assigned to the requested user.

> **FLEXIBILITY** If you're astute, you may have caught the fact that we're using `$routeParams` to resolve the user property in the route configuration object, while using it in the `UserCtrl` as well to get the same value. This is strictly to illustrate the versatility and variations that are available in AngularJS. In production, we'd choose the best option and use that exclusively.

What happens if a value returned by `resolve` makes a remote server call and that call fails? If the return value of a route `resolve` property is a promise, a `$routeChange-Success` event is fired when the promise is resolved and `ngView` will instantiate the appropriate controller and render the template. If the promise is rejected, then a `$routeChangeError` event is fired and additional handling is necessary.

7.4.1   *Review*

You've just learned how to use `resolve` in a route definition to create a route dependency that will be injected into our route's controller. In our example, we called the `UsersModel` to fetch a user's information and deliver it to the `UserCtrl` as a user dependency. We also used the `StoriesModel` to deliver all of the stories to the `UserCtrl` as a stories dependency.

7.5 Route events

At this point, Angello is really starting to take shape in terms of functionality, but there are some UX things that we can do to make the experience better. We have a `LoadingService` that sets flags on whether or not the application is loading, which is bound to a modal preloader. This provides the viewer with a visual cue that Angello is doing something behind the scenes, as shown in figure 7.4.

Figure 7.4 Using route events to give the viewer appropriate visual feedback

We want to show the loading animation when Angello is changing from one route to another. We can accomplish this by listening for the `$routeChangeStart` and `$routeChange-Success` events. We'll set loading to true when the route starts to change, and set it to false when the route change is completed.

Let's dig into the code to see how this would be accomplished:

> Since this behavior exists across the entire application, we put it in the run block of the module. We inject $rootScope to listen for the route change events and LoadingService to handle the state of the loading modal.

> We attach an event listener for the $routeChangeStart event via $rootScope.$on.

> In our event handler, we set loading to true on the LoadingService.

> We attach an event listener for the $routeChangeSuccess event via $rootScope.$on.

> And now we set loading to false to hide the modal.

```
// client/src/angello/Angello.js
myModule.run(function ($rootScope, LoadingService) {
    $rootScope.$on('$routeChangeStart', function (e, curr, prev) {
        LoadingService.setLoading(true);
    });

    $rootScope.$on('$routeChangeSuccess', function (e, curr, prev) {
        LoadingService.setLoading(false);
    });
});
```

7.5.1 Review

You just learned how to use `$routeChangeStart` and `$routeChangeSuccess` to detect when Angello was changing from one view to another. This allowed us to set a property on `LoadingService` to show and hide a modal while the new route was being loaded and resolved.

7.6 Testing

You're beginning to see a pattern in testing: you define variables global to the test, inject necessary modules, inject the required dependencies, assign dependencies to your global variables, and then test some assertions. Testing a route follows the same pattern; you define your globals (including a variable that holds the URL of the route you want to test), and you inject the `$location`, `$route`, `$templateCache`, and `$rootScope` dependencies, assigning them for use later in the module. The one thing worth mentioning is that you have to manually grab the correct template and put it in the `$templateCache` before you can proceed:

```
client/tests/specs/routes/UserRoute.spec.js
describe('User Route', function () {
    var $route,
        $rootScope,
        $location,
        url = 'login';

    // Inject and assign the $route and $rootScope services.
    // Put the template in template cache.

    beforeEach(module('Angello'));

    beforeEach(inject(function
        (_$location_, _$route_, $templateCache, _$rootScope_) {
        $route = _$route_;
        $rootScope = _$rootScope_;
        $location = _$location_;

        $templateCache.put('src/angello/login/tmpl/login.html', '');
    }));
});
```

Now all we need to do is test whether our configuration is correct. We do this by using `$location` to navigate to our URL, invoking a digest cycle with `$rootScope.$digest`, and then asserting that the current route has the same `controller`, `controllerAs`, and `templateUrl` properties that we defined on the route in the first place.

```
client/tests/specs/routes/UserRoute.spec.js

describe('User Route', function () {

    //...

    it('should be defined with
        correct controller and templateUrl', function() {
        $location.path(url);
        $rootScope.$digest();

        expect($route.current.controller).toEqual('LoginCtrl');
        expect($route.current.controllerAs).toEqual('login');
        expect($route.current.templateUrl)
            .toEqual('src/angello/login/tmpl/login.html');
    });
});
```

7.7   Best practices

Your route structure should look like your file structure. In chapter 2, we said that a good file structure will often reflect the code structure, and this holds true for routes as well. If a developer can look at your route config and see the parallels between it and the file structure, you can be certain that developer will not only be able to rapidly get up to speed on the flow of your application, but will likely actually enjoy working on your application. Happy developers are productive developers. 'Nuff said.

Use resolve to get resources via $routeParams whenever possible. In the interest of keeping fat models and skinny controllers, we like to interact with `$routeParams` within the confines of a `resolve` block within a particular route. This isn't a hard-and-fast rule, it's just the way we like to do things.

> ### Multiple views and side views
>
> Using `ngRoute` helped us build a solid foundation for routing in AngularJS. But it doesn't support features like multiple views and nested views. The go-to router for advanced routing is `ui.router`, and we strongly suggest learning how to use it. Visit https://github.com/angular-ui/ui-router/wiki to learn more.

7.8 Summary

Let's review what we've covered in this chapter:

- The main AngularJS components that facilitate routings are `$routeProvider`, `$route`, `$routeParams`, and `ngView`.
- `$routeProvider` is responsible for setting up the route definitions and does this in the config block of the application module.
- `$route` is responsible for watching `$location.path` and finding matches with preexisting route definitions. Once a route has been matched, `$route` hands off the route configuration object to `ngView` to handle the setup.
- `ngView` is responsible for loading the template for the route, compiling the template with the route's controller, and resolving dependencies defined in the `resolve` object map.
- URL parameters are mapped to variables and made available through the `$routeParams` service.

Practically speaking, we've set up multiple routes within Angello that allow us to navigate to various views such as the dashboard view, user view, storyboard view, and so on. You learned to pass values such as `userId` from one view to another, as in the case of navigating from the `users` view to the `user` view. We also used `resolve` to predetermine if a viewer was logged in and respond appropriately, as well as send in user information and stories to the `user` view. And finally, we used `$routeChangeStart` and `$routeChangeSuccess` to show and hide our loading modal in between route changes.

Forms and validations

8

This chapter covers

- How AngularJS extends form elements
- Handling validations with AngularJS
- Setting up validations on an element
- Displaying validation errors and Angello

Angello has turned into a fairly full-featured application at this point, but there's a major piece of functionality that we need to add. What happens if a user submits a new story and they haven't filled in any information? What happens if we want to limit the length of the title field? We need to be able to enforce conformity on the data that goes into the application, as well as provide instant feedback to the user when something is amiss. This is where forms and validations play a crucial role in developing an AngularJS application.

In this chapter we'll explore how AngularJS extends HTML forms so that you can bind the form and its form elements to $scope. We'll use that relationship to enable and disable the ability to submit a form. We'll then show how to set validations on individual form elements, and finally display feedback to the user based on their input.

8.1 The big picture: AngularJS form validation

When adding form validations to a project such as Angello, you start with the `form` object itself and then work inwards to the input and other form elements that are the children of this `form` object. We'll outline the actual states that the form takes during input within the controller, and then use those states to show meaningful feedback in our view. See figure 8.1.

8.1.1 Extending HTML form elements

AngularJS is incredibly powerful when it comes to creating custom HTML elements, but it also has the ability to override and extend existing HTML elements. In the case of form validation, AngularJS comes with a `form` directive that extends the standard HTML form elements and creates an instance of `FormController` to keep track of state within the form.

Continuing on with our Angello application, the first step to setting up validations on our form is to give it a name via the `name` attribute. The name that we use will be published on the corresponding controller so that we can monitor the various states of the form:

```
<!-- client/src/angello/storyboard/tmpl/storyboard.html -->
<form name="storyboard.detailsForm"></form>
```

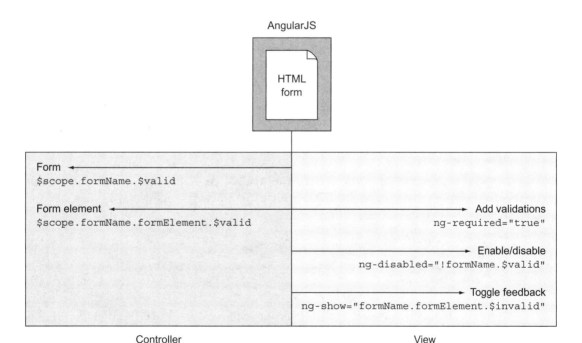

Figure 8.1 The big picture

The `form` object comes with a few predefined states that allow you to make decisions on what actions you want to allow. These states are as follows:

- `$pristine`—This Boolean flag indicates that the form is unmodified.
- `$dirty`—This Boolean flag indicates that the form has been modified.
- `$valid`—This Boolean flag indicates that the form is in a valid state.
- `$invalid`—This Boolean flag indicates that the form is in an invalid state.
- `$error`—This object contains all the validations on a form and whether they're valid or invalid.
- `$touched`—This Boolean flag indicates that a control has lost focus.

In our Angello application, we want to prevent the user from submitting a story if there's something wrong with the form. We'll bind the `ng-disabled` directive to `!storyboard.detailsForm.$valid` so that `ng-disabled` is `true` when `detailsForm` is *not* valid:

```html
<!-- client/src/angello/storyboard/tmpl/storyboard.html -->
<div ng-if="storyboard.currentStory">
    <button class="btn btn-default" ng-click="storyboard.updateCancel()">
        Cancel
    </button>
    <button class="btn pull-right btn-default"
            ng-disabled="!storyboard.detailsForm.$valid"
            ng-click="storyboard.updateStory()">Update</button>
</div>
<div ng-if="!storyboard.currentStory">
    <button class="btn pull-right btn-default"
            ng-disabled="!storyboard.detailsForm.$valid"
            ng-click="storyboard.createStory()">New Story</button>
</div>
```

Since we disable the buttons when the form is in an invalid state, the user can't submit until the form is in a valid state.

8.1.2 Adding validations

Insert awesome form validations here (no, really). We'll use a great little sub-module called ngMessages to help us display our error messages. As usual, we just need to include the angular-messages.min.js file in boot.js:

```js
// client/assets/js/boot.js
//...
{ file:'//cdnjs.cloudflare.com/ajax/libs/angular.js/1.3.3/angular-
    messages.min.js' },
//...
```

And now that ngMessages is available to our application, we need to include the sub-module in Angello.js:

```js
// client/src/angello/Angello.js
var myModule = angular.module('Angello',
    [
```

```
//...
'ngMessages',
//...
]);
```

Now that we have ngMessages and the form object available, we'll add validations for the individual form elements. The FormController not only makes the form object available, but exposes the individual form elements via a formName.inputFieldName.property format.

Taking the inputTitle input element as our first example, we can tell if it's invalid by hooking up the ngMessages directive to the storyboard.detailsForm.inputTitle.$error object:

```html
<!-- client/src/angello/storyboard/tmpl/storyboard.html -->
<input class="form-control" type="text" id="inputTitle" name="inputTitle"
        placeholder="Title" ng-model="storyboard.editedStory.title">

<div class="alert alert-warning"
    ng-messages="storyboard.detailsForm.inputTitle.$error"
    ng-if="storyboard.showMessages('inputTitle')">

    <div ng-message="required">
        <small>Required!</small>
    </div>
</div>
</div>
```

This code has two main parts. First, we create a div with classes alert and alert-warning, define the ng-messages directive on it, and feed it the storyboard.detailsForm.inputTitle.$error object. Then we create a child div, define an ng-message directive on it, and feed it the name of the error that we want to validate against. At this point, we can put any HTML inside of this div and it will show up when the inputTitle field is invalid.

It's not uncommon for a field to initialize to an invalid state on load because the field may be empty, which would violate a required or minimum length requirement. It's a bit jarring to show an error message before a user has had a chance to input any information, and so this is why we also bind to the storyboard.showMessages method. By using ng-if="storyboard.showMessages('inputTitle')" in conjunction with ngMessages, we tell AngularJS to only show the error container after the user has left the field and it's invalid:

```javascript
// client/src/angello/storyboard/controllers/StoryboardController.js
angular.module('Angello.Storyboard')
    .controller('StoryboardCtrl',
        function($scope, $log, StoriesModel, UsersModel,
                STORY_STATUSES, STORY_TYPES) {
            //...
            storyboard.showMessages = function (field) {
                return storyboard.detailsForm[field].$touched
                    && storyboard.detailsForm[field].$invalid;
            };
            //...
        });
```

storyboard.showMessages takes a form field and returns true or false based on the value of some attribute(s) of that field. We could have just as easily put this logic directly into the ng-if; however, once we start adding more than one logic statement to an HTML attribute, the HTML starts to get ugly. It's better to keep that logic in the controller and thus keep your HTML clean and pretty.

Now that we know how to monitor the state of detailsForm, we start adding validations to the individual form elements to make sure that our data is in a format that we want.

NG-REQUIRED

The first issue that we want to address is to ensure that users can't submit a user story without filling in all of the required fields. For instance, we need to make sure that every story has a title (see figure 8.2).

We can accomplish this with ng-required="true" or simply required:

Figure 8.2   This field is required.

```
<!-- client/src/angello/storyboard/tmpl/storyboard.html -->
<label class="control-label" for="inputTitle">*Title</label>
<input class="form-control" type="text" id="inputTitle" name="inputTitle"
    placeholder="Title" ng-model="storyboard.editedStory.title"
    ng-required="true">
```

We set ng-required="true" on the inputTitle field. This completes our required validation; we're now able to display a formatted error message when someone leaves the title field blank.

NG-MINLENGTH

We also want to make sure that the user has submitted a title that's descriptive, and so we'll enforce that with a minimum length requirement (see figure 8.3).

We can set a minimum length requirement using ng-minlength:

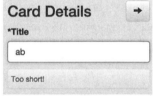

Figure 8.3   The input is too short.

```
<!-- client/src/angello/storyboard/tmpl/storyboard.html -->
<label class="control-label" for="inputTitle">*Title</label>
<input class="form-control" type="text" id="inputTitle" name="inputTitle"
    placeholder="Title" ng-model="storyboard.editedStory.title"
    ng-required="true" ng-minlength="3">

<div class="alert alert-warning"
    ng-messages="storyboard.detailsForm.inputTitle.$error"
    ng-if="storyboard.showMessages('inputTitle')">

    <div ng-message="required">
        <small>Required!</small>
    </div>
    <div ng-message="minlength"> <small>Too short!</small> </div>
</div>
```

In this case, we set a minimum length requirement to 3; then we add another child div with the ng-message directive to the ng-messages div, and voila! We have another error message ready to use.

Custom and asynchronous validation

Sometimes you want more complex validation than Angular can accomplish. Not to worry, you can build your own custom validation directives. The only main difference is that you need to include the ngModel module into your directive. Say, for example, that you want to see if a user's input is an integer or not. Let's take an example straight from the AngularJS docs:

```javascript
// Javascript
var INTEGER_REGEXP = /^\-?\d+$/;
app.directive('integer', function() {
    return {
        require: 'ngModel',
        link: function(scope, elm, attrs, ctrl) {
            ctrl.$validators.integer
                = function(modelValue, viewValue) {
                if (ctrl.$isEmpty(modelValue)) {
                    // consider empty models to be valid
                    return true;
                }
                if (INTEGER_REGEXP.test(viewValue)) {
                    // it is valid
                    return true;
                }
                // it is invalid
                return false;
            };
        }
    };
});
```

```html
// HTML
<input type="number" ng-model="size" name="size"
    min="0" max="10" integer />{{size}}<br />
<span ng-show="form.size.$error.integer">
 The value is not a valid integer!</span>
<span ng-show="form.size.$error.min
 || form.size.$error.max">
    The value must be in range 0 to 10!</span>
```

Asynchronous validations follow pretty much the same format except that you add the validator to ctrl.$asyncValidators and return a promise instead of a value. You can also show a loading message with <span ng-show="form.name.$pending .asyncValidation">Doing some asynchronous validation</span>. Actually showing the error is exactly the same process as normal.

NG-MAXLENGTH

At the same time, we want to make sure that a user doesn't enter a title that will cause layout problems because it's so long (see figure 8.4).

The converse to `ng-minlength` is `ng-maxlength`, which sets a maximum length restriction on the field.

Figure 8.4   The input is too long.

```
<!-- client/src/angello/storyboard/tmpl/storyboard.html -->
<label class="control-label" for="inputTitle">*Title</label>
<input class="form-control" type="text" id="inputTitle" name="inputTitle"
       placeholder="Title" ng-model="storyboard.editedStory.title"
       ng-required="true" ng-minlength="3" ng-maxlength="30">

<div class="alert alert-warning"
    ng-messages="storyboard.detailsForm.inputTitle.$error"
    ng-if="storyboard.showMessages('inputTitle')">

    <!-- ... -->
    <div ng-message="maxlength"> <small>Too long!</small> </div>
</div>
```

We want to make sure that `inputTitle` is not longer than 30 characters, so we'll add `ng-maxlength="30"` to the `inputTitle` field. Then, as before, we'll add the div with the ng-message directive bound to the `maxlength` error.

8.1.3   *Form validation and CSS*

Up to this point, we've primarily used the state of `detailsForm` to alter the DOM structure in terms of what we show to the user. AngularJS also adds a corresponding CSS class to the form element, depending on its current state. This gives you the ability to define custom styles in your CSS that determine the look and feel of your form elements.

AngularJS adds the following classes, among others:

- `.ng-valid {}`
- `.ng-invalid {}`
- `.ng-pristine {}`
- `.ng-dirty {}`

So if you wanted a particular shade of red to style the element when it was invalid or a particular green when it was valid, you'd add the following styles:

```
/* client/assets/css/angello.css */
form.ng-dirty input.ng-invalid {
    border: 1px solid #B02B2C;
}

form.ng-dirty input.ng-valid {
    border: 1px solid #6BBA70;
}
```

And the rendered HTML for an element would look like this:

```
<!-- angello/storyboard/tmpl/storyboard.html -->
<input class="form-control ng-pristine ng-invalid ng-invalid-required
              ng-valid-minlength ng-valid-maxlength ng-touched"
       type="text" id="inputTitle" name="inputTitle"
       placeholder="Title" ng-model="storyboard.editedStory.title"
       ng-required="true" ng-minlength="3" ng-maxlength="30">
```

Note that there are actually styles for the individual states of the form, if you really want to get explicit in your styling.

8.1.4   *Form validation, $setPristine, and $setUntouched*

There's one more practical detail that we'll cover in our Angello application, since it pertains to forms and validation. As a user goes through the detailsForm and inputs information, the detailsForm object is constantly updating in response to the correctness of the input at that moment. When the user is finished inputting data, how do we set the form back to its original, pristine, and untouched state?

The way to do this is to call $setPristine and $setUntouched on the form element on the $scope reference:

```
// client/src/angello/storyboard/controllers/StoryboardController.js
storyboard.resetForm = function () {
    storyboard.currentStory = null;
    storyboard.editedStory = {};

    storyboard.detailsForm.$setPristine();
    storyboard.detailsForm.$setUntouched();
};
```

In this case, we want to set detailsForm back to a pristine, untouched state when we reset the form in the StoryboardCtrl, so we call storyboard.detailsForm.$set-Pristine() and storyboard.detailsForm.$setUntouched().

8.2   *Testing*

Testing a form is a lot like testing a directive in that you have to get an HTML template and compile it with your scope. In order to load your templates without initiating HTTP requests, you need to install karma-ng-html2js-preprocessor. Instructions for doing this are in appendix A.

First off, we create our top-level variables, include the Angello.Storyboard module, and include the Angello.Templates module so we have access to our templates. Next, we need to mock out an all method on the UsersModel and StoriesModel services. We have to return a promise from these methods because the controller calls a .then method after them:

```
client/tests/specs/forms/StoryboardForm.spec.js
describe('Storyboard form', function() {
    var scope, ctrl;
```

```
beforeEach(module('Angello.Storyboard'));
beforeEach(module('Angello.Templates'));

beforeEach(inject(function($q, $rootScope, $controller,
➥ $templateCache, $compile) {

    var UsersModel = {
        all: function() {
            var deferred = $q.defer();
            deferred.resolve({});
            return deferred.promise;
        }
    };

    var StoriesModel = {
        all: function() {
            var deferred = $q.defer();
            deferred.resolve({});
            return deferred.promise;
        }
    };
}));
});
```

Pay special attention to this part of the test. We create an instance of $rootScope and assign it to our global scope. We then create an instance of StoryboardCtrl, inject our mocked dependencies, and assign it to a global.

We can access $scope attributes within our test using ctrl because we defined the controller with the controllerAs syntax within our application. But in the template that we are including, the controller is referenced as storyboard; thus, we have to create a storyboard attribute on the scope object in our test and assign it ctrl so that when we compile the template and scope, the template has access to an object called storyboard. Otherwise, storyboard.detailsVisible would not be defined, the form would not show up in the template, and the entire test would not be possible.

The last part of setup is simply getting the template, creating an Angular element out of it, compiling the element with scope, and then triggering a digest cycle:

```
client/tests/specs/forms/StoryboardForm.spec.js
describe('Storyboard form', function() {

    //...

    beforeEach(inject(function($q, $rootScope, $controller,
    ➥ $templateCache, $compile) {

        //...

        scope = $rootScope.$new();

        ctrl = $controller('StoryboardCtrl', {
            $scope: scope,
```

```
            STORY_STATUSES: {},
            STORY_TYPES: {},
            UsersModel: UsersModel,
            StoriesModel: StoriesModel
        });

        scope.storyboard = ctrl;

        var templateHtml =
    ➥   $templateCache.get('src/angello/storyboard/tmpl/storyboard.html');
        var formElem = angular.element(templateHtml);
        $compile(formElem)(scope);

        scope.$digest()
    }));
});
```

We're nearly there! All that's left to do is test a couple of assertions. First we make sure that the form is invalid when the page is first loaded and all the fields are empty. Then we create a valid story, assign it to `ctrl.editedStory`, trigger a digest cycle so that the validations are invoked, and then make sure that the form is valid:

```
client/tests/specs/forms/StoryboardForm.spec.js
describe('Storyboard form', function() {

    //…

    it('should be invalid by default', function() {
        expect(ctrl.detailsForm.$invalid).toBeTruthy();
    });

    it('should be valid with populated fields', function() {
        ctrl.editedStory = {
            title: 'Title',
            status: 'To Do',
            type: 'Enhancement',
            reporter: 'Lukas Ruebbelke',
            assignee: 'Brian Ford'
        };

        scope.$digest();

        expect(ctrl.detailsForm.$valid).toBeTruthy();
    });
});
```

> **Using ng-model-options**
> By default, Angular models update immediately when a user provides input (usually by typing). You can change that in Angular 1.3 by adding an `ng-model-options` attribute to the form control that you want to modify. For example, if you want to update the model when a user leaves the control, you could add `ng-model-options="{ updateOn: 'blur' }"` to the form control.

Nesting forms

HTML doesn't allow you to nest forms natively. In order to show proper error messages at the correct times within nested forms, you need to wrap Angular's `ng-form` directive around individual form fields. Here's an example:

```
// Hypothetical Scenario
<form name="myForm">
    <div ng-repeat="item in items"
    ➥ ng-class="{ 'has-error' : item.name.$invalid }">
        <ng-form name="itemNameForm">
            <label>Name</label>
            <input type="text" name="name"
            ➥ ng-model="item.name" required>
            <p ng-show="itemNameForm.name.$invalid">
            ➥ Name Required</p>
        </ng-form>
    </div>
</form>
```

8.3 *Best practices*

Avoid excessive use of `ng-ifs` *and* `ng-show/hides` *when customizing error messages.* We often need to do a lot of tweaking to individual input elements to get them to show up exactly when we want. This results in the repetition of many AngularJS directives, usually with multiple logic statements (such as `ng-if="this.long.condition && this.other.long.condition"`). This is sometimes unavoidable, but we recommend that you promote this logic to the controller so that your HTML stays tidy (compare the previous statement to `ng-if="shouldShowField(fieldName)"`). We can't overemphasize the value of clean code!

8.4 *Summary*

Form validation is just an extension of data binding and showing appropriate feedback to the user, depending on the state of the AngularJS `form` directive as exposed by the `FormController`. It really is that simple. Now let's take a moment to review:

- You learned how to expose the `form` element in the controller via the `name` attribute on the `form`.
- The form object has predefined states, such as `$valid`, `$invalid`, `$pristine` and `$dirty`, and `$touched`.
- Errors can be shown concisely using the `ngMessages` module along with the appropriate requirements on the elements (`ng-required`, `ng-minlength`, `ng-email`, and so on).
- You learned how to use the classes that AngularJS provides to style the different states of forms.
- A form can be set back to its original condition via the `$setPristine` and `$setUntouched` methods.

appendix A
Setting up Karma

Karma is a JavaScript test runner created by the AngularJS team. It's important to note that it's *not* a testing *framework*. It allows you to specify information about your testing environment, such as which browser(s) to use, which files to include, and so on. You then specify which testing framework you want to use (Jasmine, in our case) and write your tests using that particular framework.

Install Node.js and Node Package Manager (npm)

First things first. If you haven't yet installed Node.js, stop! Here are a couple resources to get the ball rolling:

- https://nodejs.org/download/
- You're in luck: Node.js comes with npm!

Install packages

If you *do* have Node.js and npm, welcome! First, install `karma-cli` globally so you have access to it in any directory:

```
npm install -g karma-cli
```

Next, make sure you're in the `angello` directory, and then install `karma` and save it as a dev dependency:

```
npm install karma --save-dev
```

Now, install your necessary plugins. These include the plugins for your testing framework of choice as well as any browsers that you need to integrate with. In this book, we use Jasmine as our testing framework and Chrome for our browser.

```
npm install karma-jasmine karma-chrome-launcher --save-dev
```

Initialize Karma

Now that you have all the dependencies installed, it takes only a single command in the terminal to initialize the Karma configuration:

```
karma init
```

Rather than tell you what to type, we'll show you. Figures A.1 and A.2 are screenshots detailing how Karma helps you set up your configuration file.

The first three questions are pretty straightforward. We want Jasmine as our framework, we don't want to use Require.js, and we want to use Chrome as our testing browser. The next question asks which files we want to include. We start out including any vendor files we need—in our case, the AngularJS core file along with the routing file and animation file. We also include angular-mocks.js, which aids us with writing unit tests in Angular.

We also want to include a couple of files necessary for authentication. Then we want to include all JavaScript files in any folder under src/angello, and we want to

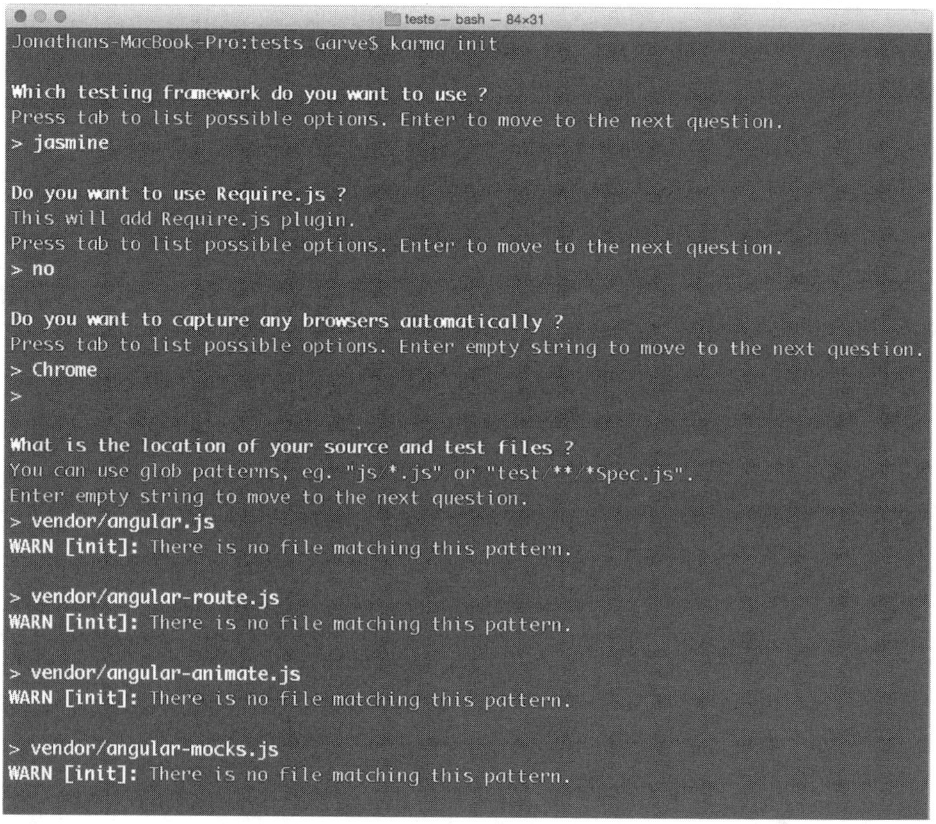

Figure A.1   Building karma.conf.js, part 1

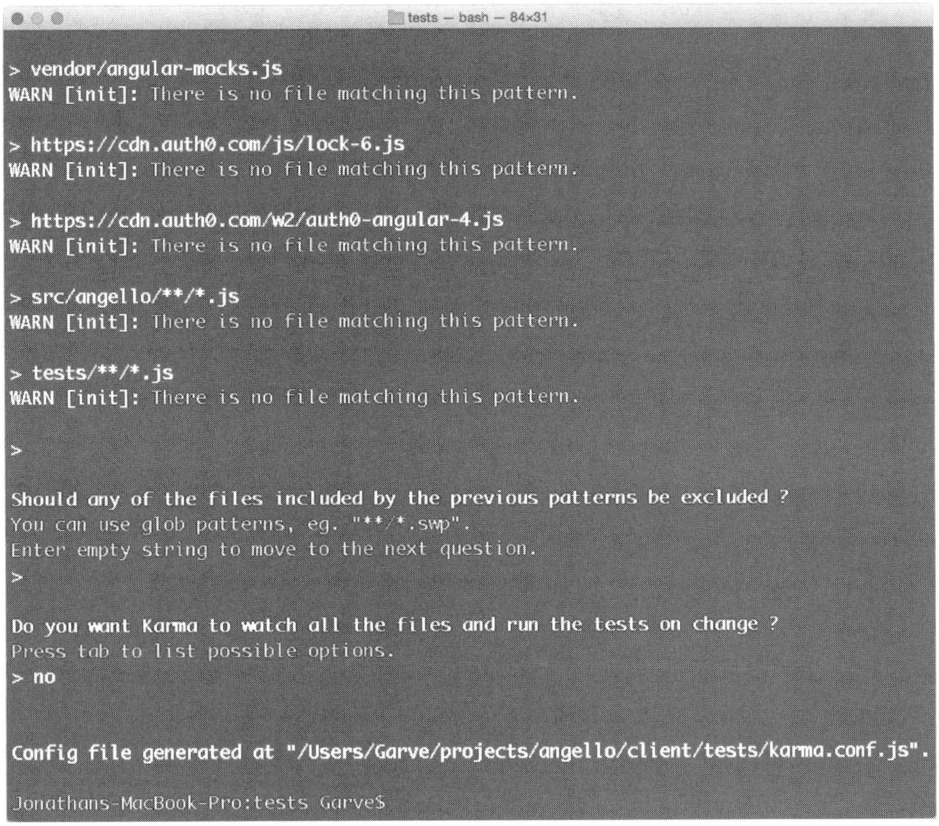

Figure A.2 Building karma.conf.js, part 2

include all JavaScript files in any folder under `tests`. For test-driven development (TDD), you'd probably want to autowatch and test each of your source files whenever they change; we decided not to do this purely for demonstration purposes.

Here's the full karma.conf.js file. Note that the *only* attribute we had to change was the `basePath`. By default it's just an empty string, but we changed it to `../` so Karma could reference the rest of the files properly.

```
// client/tests/karma.conf.js
module.exports = function (config) {
    config.set({

        // base path that will be used to resolve
        ➥    all patterns (eg. files, exclude)
        basePath: '../',


        // frameworks to use
```

```
    // available frameworks:
➡      https://npmjs.org/browse/keyword/karma-adapter
    frameworks: ['jasmine'],


    // list of files / patterns to load in the browser
    files: [
        'vendor/angular.js',
        'vendor/angular-route.js',
        'vendor/angular-animate.js',
        'vendor/angular-mocks.js',
        'https://cdn.auth0.com/js/lock-6.js',
        'https://cdn.auth0.com/w2/auth0-angular-4.js',
        'src/angello/**/*.js',
        'tests/**/*.js'
    ],


    // list of files to exclude
    exclude: [],


    // preprocess matching files before serving them to the browser
    // available preprocessors:
➡      https://npmjs.org/browse/keyword/karma-preprocessor
    preprocessors: {},


    // test results reporter to use
    // possible values: 'dots', 'progress'
    // available reporters: https://npmjs.org/browse/keyword/karma-
reporter
    reporters: ['progress'],


    // web server port
    port: 9876,


    // enable / disable colors in the output (reporters and logs)
    colors: true,


    // level of logging
    // possible values: config.LOG_DISABLE ||
➡      config.LOG_ERROR || config.LOG_WARN ||
             ➡     config.LOG_INFO || config.LOG_DEBUG
    logLevel: config.LOG_INFO,


    // enable / disable watching file and executing
➡      tests whenever any file changes
    autoWatch: false,
```

```
        // start these browsers
        // available browser launchers:
    ➥    https://npmjs.org/browse/keyword/karma-launcher
        browsers: ['Chrome'],


        // Continuous Integration mode
        // if true, Karma captures browsers, runs the tests and exits
        singleRun: false
    });
};
```

Use Karma

Now all you need to do is run `karma start --single-run` from the `client/tests` folder or run `karma start --single-run path/to/karma.conf.js` from any other folder. Another nifty trick is to specify a script in your `package.json` file so that npm can actually run tests for you.

```
// package.json
{

    //...

    "scripts": {
        "test": "karma start --single-run
    ➥      --browsers Chrome client/tests/karma.conf.js"
    },

    //…
}
```

Here we define a `test` script that evaluates to a Karma command. Just run `npm test` anywhere in your project, and Karma will do a single pass on your tests. Go ahead: try it!

appendix B
Setting up a Node.js server

You can run Angello one of two ways: with Firebase or Node.js. We'll show you how to install Node.js and integrate it with Angello.

Install Node.js (with Node Package Manager, a.k.a. npm) and MongoDB

If you don't have Node.js and npm, here are a few resources to get you started:

- Git (http://git-scm.com/)
- Node.js (https://nodejs.org/download/)
- You're in luck: Node.js comes with npm!

To install MongoDB, go to http://docs.mongodb.org/manual/installation/ and follow the directions for your specific platform.

Initialize the repo

Go to your terminal and run the following commands (after you've installed Git and Node.js):

```
cd <your-projects-folder>
git clone https://github.com/angularjs-in-action/angello-express-api
cd angello-express-api
npm install
node server.js
```

In a nutshell, these commands download a copy of the server code into your projects directory, install all of the necessary dependencies, and start up a server listening on http://localhost:4000.

> **NOTE** The code running on localhost:4000 is not the main Angello app; it's only the back-end API that provides data persistence. If you want to set up the main app locally, please see appendix D.

Update EndpointConfigService.js

If you haven't already cloned the main Angello app, you can do so by running the following commands in your terminal:

```
cd <your-projects-directory>
git clone https://github.com/angularjs-in-action/angello
cd angello
```

A note about Auth0

By default, the API you just initialized has an .env file that contains the following two lines: AUTH0_CLIENT_ID and AUTH0_CLIENT_SECRET. These values come prepopulated from an account that we set up with Auth0. Also, in the config block of Angello.js in the Angello app, you'll find an initializer (currently starting at line 64) that looks like the following:

```
// client/src/angello/Angello.js
// Auth0 Authentication
authProvider.init({
    domain: 'angello.auth0.com',
    clientID: 'Fq8hKAkghu45WpnqrYTc6dbvXhBUdP7l'
});
```

If you want to create your own account and play with Auth0, go to https://auth0.com/ and create an account. Then substitute your Client ID and Client Secret for the AUTH0_CLIENT_ID and AUTH0_CLIENT_SECRET in the .env file in the API and substitute your Client ID and domain for the clientID and domain in the Angello.js file in the main Angello app.

Setting up a Firebase server

Angello comes with Firebase already set up. However, we *strongly* encourage you to set up your own account with Firebase so you can view and manipulate all your data.

Set up an account with Firebase

Go to https://www.firebase.com/ and click Start Hacking. Once you have registered, you'll be taken to your brand-new dashboard.

Create your first app

On the left side of your dashboard, you'll see a form for creating new apps. Fill it out with a name like my-first-angello (or some other descriptive name that strikes your fancy). Then click Create New App to breathe life into your new application!

Bootstrap your Firebase app to Angello

If you haven't yet downloaded the code for Angello, head on over to appendix D to get set up.

Once you have the code, go back to your browser and view your created app. Click the provided Firebase URL; this will take you to your app's view. Copy the entire URL in your address bar; then open EndpointConfigService.js, find the end-PointMap object, and update its URI property to your Firebase URL. *Make sure there's a trailing slash at the end.* In the same file, make sure that .constant ('CURRENT_BACKEND', 'firebase') (line three as of this writing) is uncommented and .constant('CURRENT_BACKEND', 'node') (line two as of this writing) is commented out. Start up the Angello app, create a user and a story, and then go back to your Firebase URL and see the magic that is real-time data!

A note about Auth0

By default, in the `config` block of Angello.js in the Angello app, you'll find an initializer (currently starting at line 64) that looks like the following:

```
// client/src/angello/Angello.js
// Auth0 Authentication
authProvider.init({
    domain: 'angello.auth0.com',
    clientID: 'Fq8hKAkghu45WpnqrYTc6dbvXhBUdP7l'
});
```

If you want to create your own account and play with Auth0, go to https://auth0.com/, create an account, and then substitute your Client ID and domain for the defaults we provide here.

appendix D
Running the app

Running the app is a super-simple process. To start off, you'll need Git (http://git-scm.com/) and, if you don't have a local web server, you'll need Node.js and npm (https://nodejs.org/download/).

Get the code

Once you have Git installed, go to your terminal and run the following:

```
cd <your-projects-folder>
git clone https://github.com/angularjs-in-action/angello
cd angello
```

These commands will download all of the code for the front-end app into your projects folder.

Start the server

If you have a local web server that you use, simply serve the client directory of the project. If you don't, run the following commands in your terminal. Make sure you have installed Node.js and npm and that you are in the angello directory you just cloned.

```
npm install -g serve
serve client/
```

These commands install the serve package on your system globally and then serve the client directory of the Angello application for your viewing pleasure.

View the app

You now have a local copy of Angello running on http://localhost:3000. Simply navigate to that URL in your favorite browser and you will be greeted with an authentication page where you can create an account and use the app!

index

RELATED MANNING TITLES

Getting MEAN
with Mongo, Express, Angular, and Node
by Simon Holmes

ISBN: 9781617292033
375 pages, $44.99
June 2015

Node.js in Action, Second Edition

by Mike Cantelon, Alex Young, Marc Harter,
T.J. Holowaychuk, Nathan Rajlich

ISBN: 9781617292576
500 pages, $49.99
January 2016

Express.js in Action

by Evan Hahn

ISBN: 9781617292422
245 pages, $39.99
September 2015

MongoDB in Action, Second Edition

by Kyle Banker, Peter Bakkum, Shaun Verch,
Douglas Garrett, Tim Hawkins

ISBN: 9781617291609
375 pages, $44.99
October 2015

For ordering information go to www.manning.com

Node.js in Practice

by Alex Young and Marc Harter

ISBN: 9781617290930
424 pages, $49.99
December 2014

Secrets of the JavaScript Ninja,
Second Edition

by John Resig, Bear Bibeault, Josip Maras

ISBN: 9781617292859
375 pages, $44.99
February 2016

JavaScript Application Design
A Build First Approach

by Nicolas Bevacqua

ISBN: 9781617291951
344 pages, $39.99
January 2015

jQuery in Action, Third Edition

by Bear Bibeault, Yehuda Katz, Aurelio De Rosa

ISBN: 9781617292071
475 pages, $44.99
August 2015

For ordering information go to www.manning.com

YOU MAY ALSO BE INTERESTED IN

D3.js in Action

by Elijah Meeks

ISBN: 9781617292118
352 pages, $44.99
February 2015

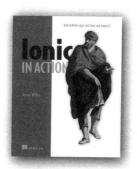

CORS in Action
Creating and consuming cross-origin APIs
by Monsur Hossain

ISBN: 9781617291821
240 pages, $49.99
October 2014

Ionic in Action
Hybrid Mobile Apps with Ionic and AngularJS
by Jeremy Wilken

ISBN: 9781633430082
325 pages, $44.99
August 2015

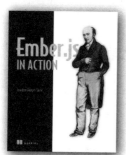

Ember.js in Action

by Joachim Haagen Skeie

ISBN: 9781617291456
264 pages, $44.99
May 2014

For ordering information go to www.manning.com